The Story of
Calder Vale
and Oakenclough

The Lappet
and other Victorian Works

by Jack Wilcock

1998

This work is dedicated to my younger daughter Gillian

I wish to record my appreciation to the following :
Frank Calderbank
Peter Guy
David Jackson
Michael Mullett
Bob Quick
Edward Robinson
Arnold Whitehead
Harris Reference Library, Preston
Lancashire Record Office
Lappet Manufacturing Company
North West Water for a kind welcome to the reservoir site

For photographic credits see page 7

The Lappet and other Victorian Works :
The Story of Calder Vale and Oakenclough
Text Copyright © Jack Wilcock 1998

Printed by Colin Cross Printers, Garstang

Published by Jack Wilcock

ISBN 0 9531719 1 4

Foreword by David Jackson, Managing Director of the Oakenclough Paper Mill, 1968 - 1971

In a recent volume the author gathered together many historical facts and much anecdotal evidence of the history of this area : Oakenclough and Calder Vale. I put the names in this order because it was from 'the Cloo' that Calder Vale was created, and, although inextricably linked, the 'Cloo-ites' and the 'Valers' have always sustained a friendly rivalry.

As a result of his previous publication, Jack Wilcock has been persuaded by Bob Quick, the present Managing Director of the Lappet Manufacturing Company (Vale Mill), to investigate the industrial history of the cotton mills in Calder Vale more deeply; indeed the author has broadened the horizons of this task and has included other industrial and utility enterprises of this micro-geographical district.

While not claiming that what is written is unique in the context of the history of our nation - there are undoubtedly other very similar stories to be told - nevertheless this one is unique in its own right.

What is so commendable is the fact that it has been done, before so much of the information which has been accumulated becomes faded by time, and the passing of those 'in the know'.

My great-great-grandfather bought the paper mill at Oakenclough in 1827, and it was my privilege to serve the enterprise in the final phase of its development, and subsequently its demise, which was, to say the least, a personally traumatic experience. The cotton mills in Calder Vale suffered in similar ways over the years.

Such is progress : 'large oaks from little acorns grow', but do not last forever. What, I wonder, does the future hold in store for the locality?

The author has, through his own diligent research, utilising written evidence and word of mouth, assembled a most interesting book, which is no mean task. From his endeavours I personally have learned a lot which I did not know previously.

As a direct descendant of one of the three Jackson brothers who brought industry to the upper reaches of the river Calder in the nineteenth century, I am pleased to commend this book, which features the story, and consequences, of my various ancestors' vision and enterprise.

Clough Lodge
Strickens Lane
Oakenclough
September 1998

Contents

1. Introduction

PART 1 : COTTON

2. Once upon a time ...
3. Spinning
4. Weaving
5. Lappet Figuring
6. Calder Vale mills in the nineteenth-century
7. Vale Mill : 'The Lappet'
8. Lappet Satellites
9. Low Mill

PART 2 : PAPER

10. Paper making
11. Oakenclough Paper Mill

PART 3 : WATER

12. The water cycle
13. The Grizedale and Barnacre Reservoirs

APPENDICES

A. Notes and references
B. Bibliography
C. Cotton mill employment according to census returns (1841 - 1891)
D. Paper mill employment according to census returns (1841 - 1891)
E. Glossary

Index

Postscript : Cotton Mill Rules : circa 1847

Photographic Insert : Contents
Photographs listed in order of presentation
[*Acknowledgements in parentheses*]

i.	Lappet Headshawl	[*Lappet Manufacturing Company*]
ii.	James W Whitehead	[*Arnold Whitehead*]
iii.	Humphrey Whitehead	[*Arnold Whitehead*]
iv.	Arthur Whitehead	[*Arnold Whitehead*]
v.	Fred Whitehead	[*Arnold Whitehead*]
vi.	Barnacre Reservoirs : high level view	[**]
vii.	Barnacre Filter House : interior	[*North West Water*]
viii.	Paper Mill : aerial view	[**]
ix.	'Bag Factory' : aerial view	[*Winter & Kidson*]
x.	120 inch paper making machine	[**]
xi.	Presentation of long service awards (paper mill)	[*David Jackson*]
xii.	David Jackson	[*David Jackson*]

Front cover illustration :
    Vale Mill : 'The Lappet'   [*Frank Calderbank*]

Maps and Plans

Vale Mill : 1994	page 37
Low Mill	page 45
Paper Mill : 1912	page 57
Paper Mill : 1971	page 63
Waterworks	page 77

Logos

Lappet Manufacturing Company	page 31
Oakenclough Paper Mill	page 58

Lappet Designs   page 24

** *The compiler regrets and apologises for having failed to trace the ownership of these photographs. He begs forbearance on the part of any claimant on the grounds that the omission from this work of these pictorial records would represent a lost opportunity.*

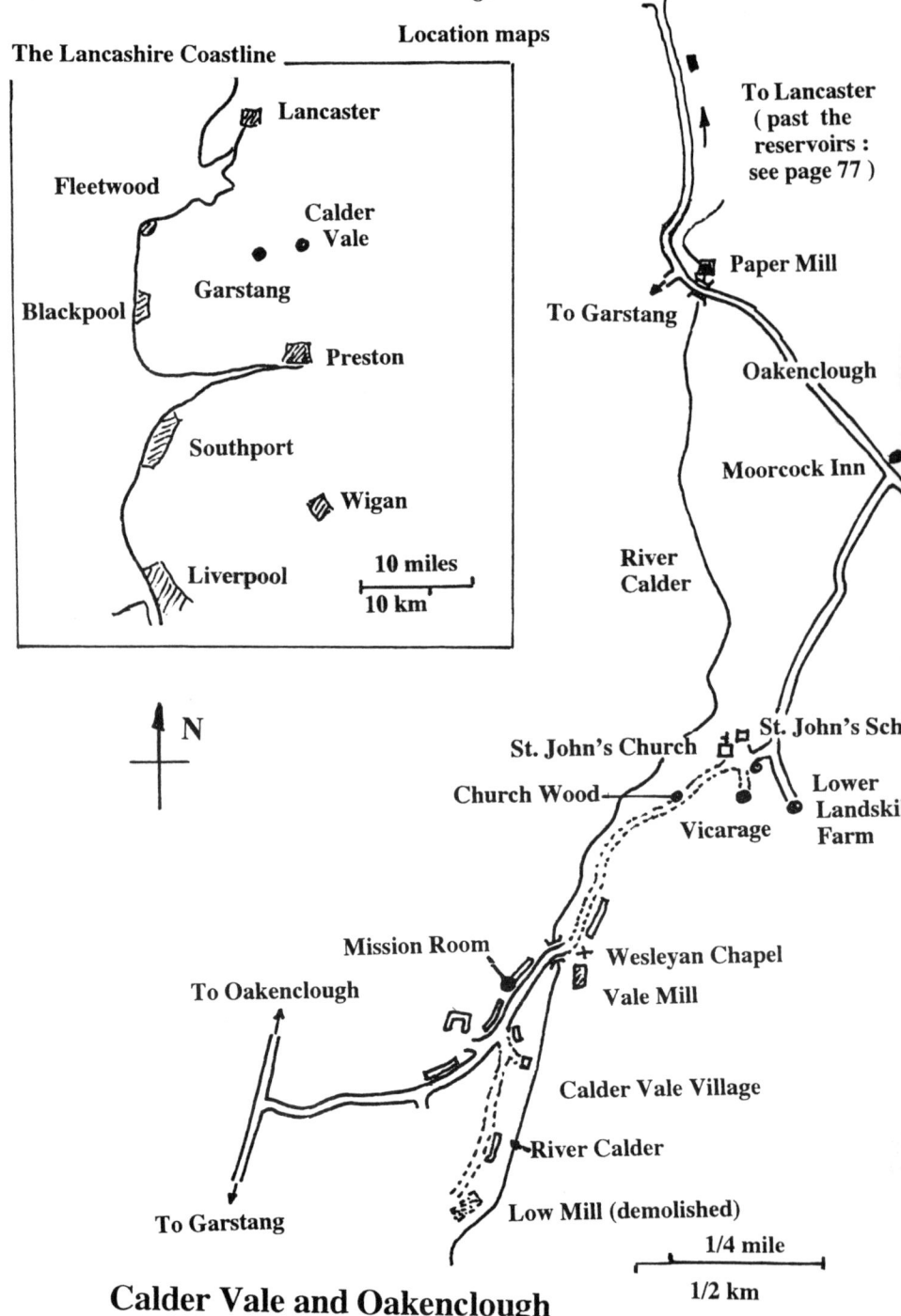

Calder Vale and Oakenclough

1. Introduction

Whilst the roots of the Industrial Revolution are firmly planted in the eighteenth century, its initial impact on society was patchy and uneven, only gaining impetus as the growth and spread of industry provided incentive for the working poor to transform their lives. The accelerating pace of invention we experience today implies that it is not yet, or is ever likely to be, a finite entity. Despite the widespread adoption of automation and mass-production techniques, labour intensive and time-honoured manufacturing methods have not been altogether ousted, but continue to provide quality items with the individual appeal sought by discerning clients.

The initial phases of the Industrial Revolution of direct concern to Calder Vale were substantially in place when the village was born in 1835. Mechanical inventions designed to speed the production of cloth and paper, and the ready availability of coal and steel, gave incentive to early nineteenth century entrepreneurs, such as the Jackson brothers (who came to the district around 1820), to become involved in supplying expanding markets. As demand for their products shifted, village viability depended upon management perception to adjust and keep up to date with current trends and techniques, and later to seek niche markets in which they could offer specialist products of high esteem.

As this study shows, success depends rather too much on outside influence ever to be certain. Consequently, of the four businesses dealt with in this book, Low Mill failed because of a contracting market, and the paper mill, though flourishing in its own right, fell victim to consortium rationalisation. As regards the other two, the water company survives by monopolising a natural resource, and the Lappet continues to prosper by delivering a quality product of unique derivation to a demanding client.

It is to commemorate the success and record the history of the Lappet enterprise that this book has been written. However, the interweaving fortunes of all four Victorian endeavours, together with their joint contribution to villagers' work prospects, demands that each one be accorded its own legitimate entry amongst the chapters which follow.

The book is designed to set the scene in general terms before concentrating on local detail. Here and there, later events bear relevance to earlier chapters. Therefore, to avoid misunderstanding, it would be as well, at the outset, to delineate the birth and early years of the small up-hill community to which this study refers.

In 1775, when the paper mill at Oakenclough began trading, the flanks of the river Calder were lined with woodland and pasture, providing a home for scattered farms and their livestock. In the 1820s, three Jackson brothers bought lands adjacent to the stream to continue with their established yeoman lifestyle. John's portion included the paper mill. When the mill owner was declared bankrupt in 1826, John took over. The other brothers, Jonathan and Richard, decided to follow his venture into industry by constructing a spinning mill one mile downstream in 1835, surrounded by cottages for their workers. Vale Mill, as it was called, thus became the focus of a brand new village aptly named Calder Vale. Twelve years later, following Richard's withdrawal, Jonathan added a weaving shed (Low Mill) and more housing to complete the industrial potential of the place. In 1886, Jonathan died, and, because of a slump in the cotton industry, his heirs opted to sell. The Fylde Waterworks Company seized the opportunity to secure the water rights. A decade of uncertainty for the two cotton mills ensued until the Liver family took possession. Spinning at Vale Mill was discontinued in favour of weaving. In the meantime, John Jackson's descendants kept the paper mill at Oakenclough in production, and this, together with the operation of recently constructed reservoirs on Barnacre Moor, provided some alternative employment for the villagers.

These introductory words will suffice to establish a starting point. Although the book is divided into three parts - cotton, paper, and water - the inter-relationship between these three industries and their contribution to village life will become apparent as the narrative unfolds.

Part 1

Cotton

Dates of Relevance

1519 'Flyer' invented by Leonardo da Vinci
1555 Saxony spinning wheel invented (incorporating 'flyer')
1725 Basile Bouchon's heald control by perforated cards
1733 John Kay's flying shuttle
1738 Lewis Paul automated the drawing process
1767 James Hargreaves' spinning jenny
1769 Richard Arkwright's water frame
1779 Samuel Crompton's spinning mule
1785 Edmund Cartwright's power loom
1794 Saw gin invented by Eli Whitney
1801 Joseph Marie Jacquard's pattern weaving
1803 William Horrocks' metal power loom
1822 Richard Roberts' power loom
1828 John Thorpe's ring spinning process
1830 Richard Roberts' self-acting mule
1833 Factory Act restricted employment of children
1835 Vale Mill constructed (for spinning)
1840 Macarthy gin introduced
1840 Preston - Lancaster railway opened
1847 Low Mill constructed (for weaving)
1847 'Ten Hours Act' restricted working hours
1850 Saturday working hours reduced
1861-65 'Cotton Panic' due to American Civil War
1886 Jonathan Jackson died; Calder Vale mills failed
1887 Low Mill bought by Blackburn company
1887 Vale Mill bought by Fylde Waterworks Company
1892 Low Mill bought by Fylde Waterworks Company
1895 Barnacre Weaving Company incorporated

1901 Vale Mill and Low Mill bought by James William Liver
1909 Lappet Manufacturing Company incorporated
1909 Low Mill sold to James W Whitehead
1914 Low Mill weaving sheds extended
1914-18 World War I
1918 Education Act ended half-time working
1924 Low Mill warping room extended
1927 Vale Mill decision to concentrate on lappet weaving
1933 Liverbird logo adopted by Vale Mill
1935 Electricity wired to Calder Vale
1938 Holidays with pay legislation
1939-45 World War II
1949 Low Mill sold to Vivian Hill
1960 Low Mill bought John Lean
1962 Low Mill ceased trading
1962 John Lean transferred to Vale Mill
1964 Vale Mill sold to Ashton Brothers
1968 Courtaulds bought Ashton Brothers
1971 Low Mill premises redundant and set for demolition
1990 Courtaulds hived textile interests into Courtaulds Textiles
1990-1991 Gulf War
1990 Lancaster dye-house opened
1990 Carlisle weaving factory opened
1991 Clitheroe hemming factory opened
1996 Vale Mill sold by Courtaulds to United Manufacturing and Trading

2. Once upon a time ...

From earliest times cotton was used for clothing in China, India, and Egypt, whereas British garments had always been woven from wool and linen. Dutch refugees were the first to introduce cotton to our shores, but it long remained a struggling industry, needing to import its cotton-wool from Levant and the West Indies, and the associated linen yarn from Hamburg or Ireland. However, when the East India Company began trading in the seventeenth century, and payment for British exports was made in a variety of the high quality cloths being produced in India at the time, demand blossomed for these cheaper, cleaner, and easily dyed materials. The Indian origin of cotton textiles is apparent from their names : calico from Calicut, muslin from Mosul.

In the years 1666 and 1678, the organised wool trade successfully lobbied Parliament to pass legislation designed to encourage wool manufacture in the kingdom, and discourage importation of linen for the purpose, by insisting that coffins be lined, and corpses be shrouded, in wool alone.

Protectionism against foreign textiles raged again when the British manufacturers of linen and wool came together to persuade Parliament to pass a statute in 1721 which imposed a penalty of £5 upon the wearer, and £20 on the seller, of any piece of calico! Despite these fines, chintz (printed calico) became such a favourite dress material for ladies that Parliament was forced to gradually relent. In 1736 calicoes manufactured in Great Britain were allowed to be sold, provided that the warp threads were linen. In 1774, printed cotton goods were legalised on payment of 3d. per yard excise duty.

The preferential woollen laws were belatedly repealed in 1814, having been ignored for many years by those willing and able to pay the fine for non-compliance. Burial clothes were often prepared long before they were needed, and there was a natural reluctance to use flannel in place of the many illegal but more attractive alternatives. In 1734, Alexander Pope versified a contemporary lady's disdain for the compulsory woollen shroud and her understandable preference to be laid out and buried in 'charming chintz and Brussels lace'.

The lifting (and flouting) of restrictions, accompanied by a surge of inventions to speed the spinning and weaving processes, gave a tremendous boost to cotton manufacture. A wide range of materials (calicoes, checks, fustians, printed linens, muslins, velveteens) came on to the market for making up into every sort of apparel, from smocks and frocks for the lower classes to the finest costumes for the dandies. From 1750 to 1791, imports of cotton-wool increased in value from £3 million to £28 million, and exports rose tenfold over the same period of time.

Heretofore, the only clothing which the working classes could afford was linsey-woolsy and other blends of wool. Linen was much too expensive. The artisan's attire was patchwork, never washed, and worn till it fell to pieces in a state of absolute filth. The ready availability of inexpensive cotton clothes heralded a dramatic change in personal habits. Now that garments could be so easily laundered and dried to retain their fresh appearance, it defied sense to put them on an unwashed body.

One of the major distinctions dividing the upper and lower classes in the eighteenth century (those who washed and those who did not) rapidly disappeared, due entirely to the introduction of cotton textiles into the community. Some historians believe that the retreat of infection, especially of the Plague after 1665, can be traced to these new standards of personal and sartorial hygiene.

3. Spinning

Just as a chain is no stronger than its weakest link, so the quality of a finished cloth is dependent on the perfection of each and every stage in its making, beginning in the far away fields where the cotton is grown and harvested. Cotton seeds must be picked at the right time, when ripe, each worker collecting some 50 kg per day.

Cotton is the fibrous growth which envelops the seed, and from which it must be separated. The seed is black and oily, a trifle smaller than the common pea, and forms three quarters of the weight. Nothing is wasted, because the kernel can be split from the husk to produce oil, and the residue turned into cattle meal.

To disengage the fibres, a gin (contraction of 'engine') is used. It works by pulling the strands through a space too narrow for the seeds to follow, but it is imperative that the fibres are not shortened or damaged in the process. Primitive gins used a large wooden and a small iron roller turned and fed by hand. Eli Whitney's saw gin, invented in 1794, improved productivity fifty-fold. What had been a comparatively unprofitable industry boomed and spread, and the southern states of the USA soon overtook other parts of the world in the production of raw cotton. In 1840, the Macarthy gin represented another major advance by substituting a 'doctor knife' for the small roller, and using a reciprocating beater knife to free the lint from the seed without injury.

Raw cotton is normally 'ginned' close by the plantation and compressed into heavy (200 kg) bales for shipment. From about 1750, Liverpool became the leading British cotton importer, and Manchester the chief market. This was because Lancashire enjoyed so many natural advantages : coal, soft water, cheap land, and ample water power, but particularly because it is blessed with just the right amount of moisture in the air to encourage the fibres to cling together as they pass through each of the many stages of manufacture.

The factory worker's first sight of cotton is in the bale, and the first task is to break it open and fluff out and clean the content using a blowing machine. The next job is carding, which uses metal combs to align and direct the fibres into a loosely packed, rather lumpy, continuous 'roving' prior to the actual spinning process.

Transforming the roving into a fine, even, durable thread is accomplished by a combination of drawing, stretching, and twisting actions. In pre-factory times this was carried out by hand by the womenfolk (hence the word 'spinster') who unleashed the rough fibre from a distaff (a cleft staff about one yard long) held under the left arm, skilfully manipulated the strands through their fingers and right hand thumb, and wound the spun yarn onto a spindle. It was, however, particularly slow and tedious, taking sixty twelve-hour working days to spin one ounce of the fine yarn used in Indian muslins. It was in India that the spinning wheel was first introduced, but it was not until 1555 that the treadle-operated Saxony wheel was invented in Nuremberg. This incorporated a 'flyer' (originally devised by Leonardo da Vinci in 1519) which twisted the yarn before winding, and spread it evenly along the bobbin.

In 1738 the English inventor Lewis Paul (of French descent) automated the drawing process by passing the raw cotton through a succession of pairs of rollers, each pair running faster than the preceding pair, so as to extend the slivers longitudinally to the degree of fineness required. Twisting and winding had to be done by hand. Twenty years later Paul built a machine with a circular frame containing fifty spindles, which did incorporate the twisting and winding actions. Although he was the originator, his machines, made of wood, were not a commercial success, and it was left to Preston-born Richard Arkwright to develop these ideas further into his 'water frame' of 1769, the first machine capable of producing cotton yarn strong enough to be used as warp in place of linen. At about the same time (1767) James Hargreaves invented his 'spinning jenny', a hand-operated machine which allowed one person to produce several threads simultaneously. Both these innovators were subjected to abuse from hand-workers fearful that machinery would rob them of their livelihoods.

However, the quest for automation continued, and, in 1779, Samuel Crompton produced his spinning mule, so called because it combined the works of Arkwright and Hargreaves into a successful hybrid. Later on, between 1825 and 1830, Richard Roberts developed a self-acting mule which improved on Crompton's design and cut operating costs by a further 15%. In 1828, John Thorpe patented a continuous ring spinning process in the USA, but the yarn quality did not suit British requirements, and so the mechanism did not cross the Atlantic until the 1860s, and was not adopted for some time even then.

It is not the purpose of the early chapters of this book to describe in detail the various mechanical motions required to create each interim result: they are indeed too many, and often quite obscure to the non-technical observer. Instead, it is the author's intention to stroll, as it were, along the factory floor, following a trail leading from inwards goods receipt to outward despatch, halting occasionally to admire a particular implement and reflect on its history.

Such a device is Crompton's mule, which could so easily have provided inspiration for a Roland Emett whimsical cartoon, with its forward, hesitation, and reverse mechanisms, bands and pulleys, release catches and twirling spindles, all working in ordered sequence. Its most spectacular feature is the outward and inward sweep of its wide wheeled carriage which pulls away at multiple yarns for drawing and twisting, and then reverses to allow the thread to be wound on to spindles in cop form for subsequent use. Meantime, minor mechanisms jiggle away to ensure that subsidiary actions occur precisely as needed.

This is no caricature, but a time-honoured example of eighteenth century practical engineering, so delicate in operation that one pound weight of cotton can be spun into yarn that will extend to over 200 miles in length, and so gentle that, even though each complete cycle lasts as little as twelve to sixteen seconds, thread breakages are relatively infrequent. The cops, removed by a 'doffer', represent the end of the spinning process, and are carted away to be readied for the weaving operation.

4. Weaving

Weaving is an age old discipline, practised in Turkey and Palestine as long ago as 5000 BC. Vertical looms were in use in 1400 BC, with the warp strung between top and bottom crossbars. Rods were used to part the warp threads so that the weft yarn could be threaded across and between to form an interlacing mesh. After each crossing, a comb like device called a reed was used to firm the weft tightly against the completed weave. Production was slow and painstaking, though patterns could be varied at the weaver's discretion. Very little change in manufacturing method took place until the Middle Ages, when the introduction of the treadle allowed weavers to work faster when creating regular designs.

Mechanisation of the process began with the flying shuttle, invented by the English weaver John Kay in 1733. Instead of traversing a shuttle with its spool of weft back and forth by hand alone, the operator pulled on ropes to fling the shuttle along a wooden channel, considerably speeding up the procedure. This increased the demand for yarn so much that its production had to be accelerated to suit, providing encouragement for James Hargreaves to develop his spinning jenny. In its turn, this increased thread production led the English clergyman Edmund Cartwright to invent his power loom in 1785, following a meeting the year before with the water frame inventor, Richard Arkwright. In 1803 William Horrocks created a metal power loom, translated into a factory item at his Manchester works by Richard Roberts in 1822.

Colour and pattern variations have always been part of the weaver's stock-in-trade. Changing shuttles to introduce different weft is one way to create a contrast, and easy enough on a hand loom, but the more versatile and usual method, better suited to power-driven looms, is to raise and lower diverse warp threads at each pick. The result is that different weft is hidden or revealed to build the desired pattern as the cloth advances through the loom. To produce the most elaborate effects a Jacquard is used. Although the apparatus took its name from Joseph Marie Jacquard's version in 1801, the principles were actually developed by other Frenchmen between 1725 and 1746.

It is now necessary to take a brief look at the nineteenth-century power loom itself and to become acquainted with its major components. To the rear is the beam, a rotating cylinder from which the many warp threads are unwound over a back rest to come forward through the machine on their way to the take up roller at the front. Each warp is led through a slot or hole in a 'heald'. A series of healds may be held in one or other of two or more vertical frames. The warp is directed through one or other of the heald frames in some kind of alternative manner so that as the frames are moved up and down relative to each other, warp threads are parted to form a 'shed' through which a shuttle can pass.

The shuttle contains a spool of weft, which unwinds as the shuttle passes through the shed. The healds are reversed for the shuttle to make its return journey, so that, line by line, a fabric is built up of interweaving strands. To fortify the cloth, the weft is 'beaten up' by a comb like implement called the reed, which also forms a back guide for the shuttle to run against. The warp and weft, now combined, move forward over the breast beam to be wound on to the take up roller.

A correctly timed and adjusted loom in operation is a joy to behold, but setting up is crucial, and disaster awaits the slightest deviation from the norm. The whole operation is accomplished through a co-ordinated series of movements in three roughly perpendicular planes. All motion can be related to the fore and aft position of the 'slay', which is the hinged frame carrying the reed. Tilted forward, the reed firms the weft, while the shuttle lies safely in its box and the healds can be moved up or down without hindrance. Hinged backward, the left or right hand picking arm swings energetically to propel the shuttle across the loom to its other box, two hundred times a minute. Most of the noise in the weaving shed can be ascribed to this repetitious clattering action, but other parts of the machine demand consideration too, particularly the 'shedding' devices which add pattern to the cloth by parting the warp in different combinations.

The simplest and most reliable form of shedding is provided by using cams, tappets, or barrel rollers to impart movement to particular heald frames. However these are useful only where a pattern is non-existent or its length is limited to a few picks. The engagement of these shifting devices is quite straightforward since, like the treadles they replaced, there is a direct link between each heald frame and its operating mechanism.

Basile Bouchon's idea, in 1725, to control heald position with perforated cards, permitted the production of much more complicated figuring in the fabric. The Jacquard attachment, mounted above the loom, controls individual healds, and is, therefore, able to produce large and intricate patterns. Fabrics produced by this method are, however, quite costly because of the relative slowness of the weaving technique, and the time and skill required to make the cards and ready the loom for a new motif. Perhaps for these reasons, Jacquards do not seem to have been used in the Calder Vale mills.

Much simpler and cheaper to produce, but quite effective, are dobby weaves, so called because they are produced on standard looms to which a Dobby (known also as an Index, a Witch, or a Wizard) is attached. This controls the position of heald frames by detecting perforations in blocks of wood presented to the device before each pick takes place. Because there is a limit to how many heald frames a loom can accommodate to operate satisfactorily, the resulting weaves are limited to small and repetitive geometric figures.

The heald selection device works as follows. A griffe, a knife edged horizontal bar, rises and falls for each pick, but engages only with those hooks chosen to operate heald frames. Disengaged hooks and their frames remain stationary. Selection is determined by horizontal needles, which guide the hooks, being caused to press against each succeeding pattern block as it moves into place. Where there is a hole, the needle enters by spring action; where there is no hole, the needle is held back. As a consequence, designated hooks engage the griffe, the requisite warps are displaced, and the pattern advances one pick.

Besides the heald control, the loom is equipped with additional gadgets to govern overall quality and guard against failure. These are many and varied. They include take-up devices to ensure that the cloth moves through the loom without putting undue strain on the warp threads, 'temples' to counteract a natural tendency for the weft to contract the width, and a means of forming a selvedge to strengthen the cloth edges. Since there is no better way of drawing attention to the need for corrective action than stopping the loom, two devices are particularly important. One is the fork which detects the absence of a weft thread; the other is the trigger which acts when a shuttle is out of place. Both take effect immediately to limit damage to the fabric. Guards are provided to constrain the shuttle within its design trajectory, but it is still possible for shuttles to escape. Their pointed steel noses and their unpredictable line of flight pose a serious threat of injury to anyone unlucky enough to stand in their path.

Whilst the looms occupy most of the floor space and are the major means of production, other departments in weaving manufacture are equally important. There are offices to handle management and sales and create new designs. Stores are needed to accommodate incoming raw material, pattern wheels and blocks, and spare parts. Warp threads need to be wound on to beams. Sizing may be carried out in-house, and the finished product needs to be inspected and prepared for despatch.

An air of calm efficiency pervades the quieter parts of the weaving factory, not least in the warping room. Here, workers place incoming cops of yarn on to the creel in an organised manner, in accordance with the pattern requirement, and then lead the strands over a frame to be attached in order to an empty beam. Setting up can take a whole day, but once it is accomplished, 2500 yards of thread can be wound in one hour. The full beam is very heavy, but, once installed on the loom, holds sufficient warp to last four weeks before needing to be replaced. In the despatch room, cloth-lookers inspect the finished product, piece by piece, and yard by yard. Woe betide the individual weaver of faulty goods, who risked a fine on the spot, and in extreme cases might even have been dismissed without notice.

5. Lappet Figuring

Lappet fabrics have been woven in Calder Vale since the beginning of the twentieth century, and their importance to the village economy was confirmed when the approach was made, in July 1909, to register the name 'Lappet Manufacturing Company' for the trading enterprise operating from Vale Mill. Lappets were made at Low Mill as well, but it was Vale Mill which decided to concentrate all its energy into this particular field in 1927. It is now the largest of a handful of factories in the country producing them.

Lappet weaving is a unique system of shedding, which causes extra warp threads to float transversely across the surface of the fabric, between picks, to produce spots or narrow continuous figures which run more or less into stripes. The system imitates embroidery, but the pattern is created at the same time as the normal weaving process. The end product is quite strong and durable, but is not inexpensive. The loom itself is of a standard design; the figuring is produced by additions and modifications to the slay.

Shedding of the warp for the ground fabric has been described in the previous chapter, and takes place behind the slay in the normal manner. The lappet shedding device is carried on the slay, interposed immediately forward of the reed. It is a kind of needle frame which is moved, between picks, by a system of levers, ratchets, and cams. The pattern yarns are guided around and clear of the reed, and come forward to join the other warps as each pick is completed.

The whole operation is additional to, but comparable with, that described in the previous chapter. With the slay in the forward position, the shuttles are out of action, the reed firms the weft, and the ground fabric healds are repositioned as required. The needle frame has been withdrawn clear of the cloth, and it too is moved to a new position.

Slay movement not only determines the lappet shedding, but is also used to control it. The vertical movement, a constant up-and-down routine, is easily tied to the nodding motion of the slay. The other displacement is rather more complicated, and is controlled by a stepping device which advances the pattern pick by pick.

Despite practical limitations inherent in the concept of anchoring loose threads to decorate the surface of a fabric, the range of design possibilities is legion. All the patterns produced during the several decades of Liver management at Vale Mill have been preserved and fill several large binders. A small selection is reproduced below. Many designs include two or more colours, which is a complication usually avoided.

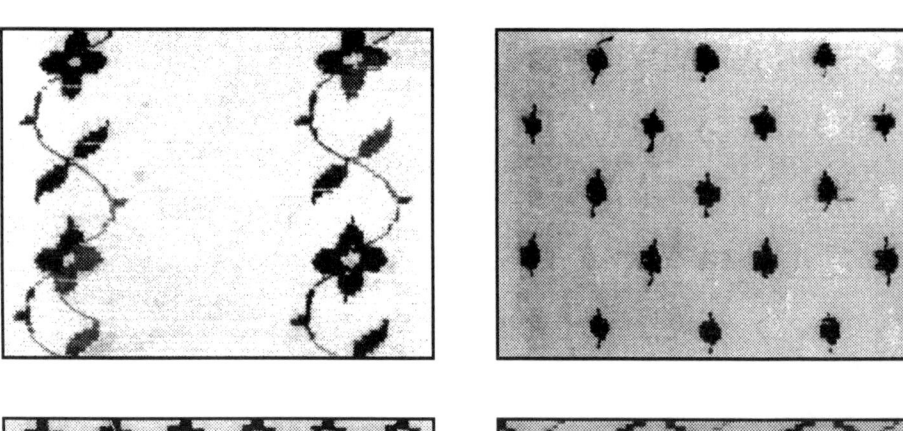

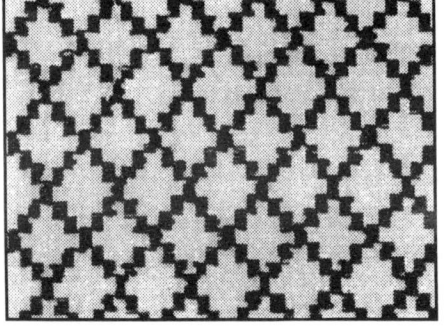

6. Calder Vale mills in the nineteenth-century

Although the hardships and living conditions of nineteenth-century workers have been studied and discussed in numerous other works, hard facts about life in tiny out-of-the-way places such as Calder Vale are not easy to come by. In earlier studies of this area, the writer has drawn on a number of contemporary sources, such as census returns, newspaper reports, parish magazines, and local authority minutes, but knowledge of life in the village remains relatively obscure, particularly in view of its disappearance from living memory. This chapter will therefore take what is known as a starting point, and make an attempt to complete the picture by adding such information as may be relevant from other communities with similar characteristics.

Following the move to Oakenclough by John Jackson about 1820, and his purchase of its paper mill in 1827, elder brother Richard and younger brother Jonathan bought up the farmland surrounding what is now known as the village of Calder Vale. Even though they were all yeoman farmers by tradition, it is possible that John's propulsion into industry incited his brothers to contemplate some parallel action.

The population was rising steadily, sales of cotton yarn and goods were accounting for just over half of Britain's overseas earnings, and a period of unrest in the cotton factories, in opposition to the mechanisation of spinning and weaving, was coming to an end. Richard Roberts had engineered Samuel Crompton's mule and Edmund Cartwright's power loom into production items. Taking all these and other developments into consideration, there can hardly have been a better time to build spinning and weaving mills. Most were placed in an urban environment, with attendant problems of overcrowding and poor sanitation. However, a model factory village had been established in rural surroundings at Styal in 1784, and it may be that its undoubted success provided some inspiration to Richard and Jonathan to do something similar when they constructed their first mill and workers' cottages to create Calder Vale in 1835. This was christened 'Vale Mill', and was fitted out with spinning machines.

The construction was of local stone, four storeys high, with power delivered to the first floor by a large water wheel positioned at the south end. Preparation and warehousing occupied the ground floor; the three floors above accommodated rows of spinning equipment. The 1841 census indicates that 110 people (two thirds of them female) worked in the mill, 90 of them engaged directly in the spinning process.

Spinning factory management structure was very simple. The owner (or general manager) looked after all matters external, and appointed an internal manager to control everything that went on inside the mill. There was an engineer to ensure provision of power to the line shaft, a carder to organise the opening of bales and all that was necessary to ensure timely delivery of bobbins of roving to the shop floor, an overlooker responsible for the entire spinning process, and a warehouseman to regulate packing and despatch. The line of demarcation between them was well understood, and, working with a minimum of communication, they all took pride in delivering what was expected of them.

In the spinning room itself, only the 'gaffer' wore boots; everyone else went barefoot to avoid slippage. All wore the flimsiest of clothes, since the atmosphere needed to be kept hot and humid. Minders looked after pairs of mules, controlled their operation, saw to all the necessary adjustments and repair of working parts like belts and pulleys, and supervised helpers who took care of four continuing actions :
  - creeling : the periodic replenishment, without interruption of manufacture, of bobbins of roving from which the yarn was spun, and which were supported on a framework called the creel,
  - piecing : a never-ending job, since on every pair of mules, five or six ends might break every minute, all to be repaired without stopping the machine,
  - doffing : the removal of cops of spun yarn, to be done in careful haste so that the machine need be halted for as short a time as possible, and
  - cleaning : needed every couple of hours or so while the machine was stopped, because fly and roving could so quickly accumulate on the working parts and spoil the yarn.

The newly constructed village, with its vacant cottages, proved particularly attractive to families with growing youngsters seeking ready employment. Of the 110 mill employees, only eighteen were aged twenty-five and over, and as many as forty-six lay within the nine to fourteen age group. The lower limit was dictated by a Factory Act of 1833, which legislated against the engagement of children younger than nine in textile factories, and restricted daily hours of work for those aged eighteen or under. Masters were also compelled to provide two hours schooling each day for children up to the age of thirteen.

Once the spinning mill was up and running, Richard withdrew from the enterprise, leaving Jonathan in charge. Business prospered sufficiently for plans to be laid to expand by building a weaving shed half a mile downstream, brought into operation in 1847. It was built in traditional style, on one storey, to ensure freedom from vibration and to keep variations in temperature and humidity to a minimum. Light entered through steeply sloped snow shedding windows, facing north so that illumination would be steady and free from sun glare. Several more cottages were constructed to house the extra workers needed. A little more is known about 'Low Mill', as it was named, because, in 1891, information about the water wheel was provided, to the government, in support of an appeal to retain the right to continue to use water from the river. It was 50 feet in diameter, and 9 feet broad, and completed two revolutions per minute, producing in excess of 75 horse power, enough to drive 200 looms 1).

Coincidentally, in 1847, Parliament brought in their 'Ten Hours Act', so that no woman, or child under the age of eighteen, should work more than ten hours a day, 58 hours a week. Eight to thirteen year olds were expected to be educated on a half time basis, and needed a certificate of school attendance for the previous week before being allowed to work. Soon afterwards (1850), trade union agitation persuaded textile employers to ease the long-established six-day work pattern by introducing an earlier finishing time on Saturday.

The 1851 census confirmed the addition of 45 houses, and a 250 person upsurge in population, which led to some overcrowding. The two mills at Calder Vale provided employment for 220 workers, two thirds of them female. There were now as many weavers as there were spinners, but, in 1861 and later, the ratio shifted so that weavers came to outnumber spinners by two to one.

When considering the daily lifestyle of nineteenth-century villagers, there is a natural tendency to make comparison between conditions now and then, but this leads inevitably to wrong interpretations and unrealistic conclusions. Their expectations were entirely different. They lived in a world where central government was only just taking its first faltering steps towards social justice, and local affairs were left in the hands of the gentry and leading figures in industry and commerce. Self-sufficiency and neighbourliness were the order of the day, and the only way a family could hope to survive.

Victorians accepted as normal what people today would see as abnormal : oil lamps, coal-fired ranges, lack of running water, sanitary inadequacies, travel restrictions, no work / no pay ; and felt no craving for improvement which did not yet exist. They came to Calder Vale because it offered employment and adequate housing. Mill hours were 6 am to 6 pm (with one and a half hours for meal breaks) from Monday to Friday, and 6 am to 2 pm (with a half hour meal break) on Saturday. Fines were levied for late arrival, with no exceptions allowed, whatever noble reason might be tendered. Very special occasions, like the consecration of St John's Anglican church in 1863 2), other major (single day) religious festivals, mill outings, or field days, merited time off, but otherwise days excused from work were few and far between, and always without pay. Good Friday was a workday, with a service in the Mission Room scheduled for 5.15 am, and surprisingly well attended 3).

Apart from the cotton panic, resulting from the American Civil War from 1861 to 1865, which obviously caused some distress in Calder Vale, because there is a newspaper report 4) lauding the Jacksons' support for their workers during this trauma, the effect of cyclic fluctuations on these mills is little publicised. The census returns do, however, show a fall in the number of mill workers from 220 in 1861 to 143 in 1881. Whether this was due to rising productivity or slackening trade one cannot tell, but it could have been the precursor to a lack of confidence in 1886, when, after Jonathan Jackson died (aged ninety-one), his heirs opted to place the mills and the village on sale 5).

Within months, Low Mill had found a buyer (its story continues in Chapter 9), but Vale Mill was not so fortunate. A predator was lurking in the shadows, in the guise of the Fylde Waterworks Company, but the mill was but a pawn, to be surrendered for its water rights. Waterworks chiefs bought the mill as individuals in 1887 6), in anticipation of an official purchase by their company in 1891 7), once an application to Parliament to divert the river water had been granted. Vale Mill lay derelict, as confirmed by Anthony Hewitson in 1900 in his book *Northward*, although the Barnacre-with-Bonds valuation list 8) records its use as a warehouse in 1896.

In March 1901, the water company finalised an 'agreement for sale and purchase of land and property at Calder Vale to Mr J Liver and conveyance thereof' 9). Even so, Vale Mill continued to be used as a warehouse, and the 1903 valuation list 10) shows Albert Harrt & Co as owner cum occupier. It was 1908 before James William Liver was listed as owner / occupier 11). On 23 July 1909, the 'Lappet Manufacturing Company' was incorporated 12), and from this date Vale Mill took on a new lease of life.

7. Vale Mill : 'The Lappet' *See page 37 for 1984 floor plan*

James William Liver (1859-1933) was no stranger to the cotton industry. Barratt Directories for Preston listed him as a cotton mill manager in 1882, progressing in 1895 to the ownership of Kent Street mill in Preston, when he began negotiations with the Fylde Waterworks Company for the purchase of the two mills in Calder Vale. In 1909, when he was fifty years old, Liver, having already divested himself of the mill at Kent Street, sold Low Mill, so that his family resources could be concentrated into Vale Mill. Articles of Association were drawn up, a mortgage arranged for the purpose, and the 'Lappet Manufacturing Company Limited' incorporated on the 23rd of July. His wife, Ruth Alice, assumed legal ownership of the premises, and his two eldest sons, Cecil and Sidney, were appointed directors 1). Looms were installed on the ground and first floors, powered by a newly acquired National gas engine. Sizing and preparation were situated on the second floor, the third harbouring the warehouse and the lappet wheel store 2).

World War I disrupted the management team. Two sons obeyed Lord Kitchener's call to arms : Cecil joined the army, and a third son, Harold, piloted DH4 aircraft in the Royal Flying Corps. Sidney remained to tend to the factory 3). At the end of the war, the mortgage was paid off, and Lappet became owner of the Vale Mill freehold. The 1918 Worrall Cotton Trade Directory advised its readers that a wide variety of fabrics was in production at Vale Mill, including the following : brocades, cambrics, dobbies, gabardines, jaconettes, lappets, plain and fancy muslins, organdies, printers, pongees, plain and fancy splits, and voiles. The majority of these light cloths were exported to Africa, India, and the East Indies.

After the Great War, working conditions improved, especially for the younger employees. A 1918 Education Act required all children to attend school until their fourteenth birthdays, and brought an end to their compulsion to work half-time. In 1919, to counter criticism from the rural district council, the mill privies were converted to water closets.

In 1927, some Northrop automatic looms, which had been used to make gabardine, were removed so that a decision to specialise in the manufacture of lappets could be implemented 4). Existing looms were adapted to weave Moroccan shawls, and their ready acceptance in the North African bazaars pioneered a drive to make and sell other designs into the Middle East. It was very soon realised that camels, used to transport goods across the desert, could not cope with standard size bales containing one hundred dozen shawls, so they were shipped in bales of fifty instead 5).

In 1933 it was becoming apparent that Lappet needed a pictorial logo, in addition to its acronymous LAPCOL trademark, to act as a mnemonic in countries less conversant with the English language and its alphabet. The natural choice, since all the directors were Liver kin, was to adopt the Liver bird. Despite its association with Liverpool, no objections were made to Vale Mill's application, and the symbol was adopted forthwith, to be set aside once for a limited period while the Courtaulds logo took precedence between 1968 and 1996.

[Not only did Vale Mill and Liverpool share this mythological bird as their icon; there is another unintentional connection between Liverpool city and Calder Vale Anglican church, in that they both acknowledge Saint John the Evangelist as their patron saint. When an anonymous artist created Liverpool's coat-of-arms 700 years ago, he was supposed to portray an eagle, the symbol for Saint John. Instead he drew a cormorant. In its beak it carries a piece of seaweed (laver), and folklore claims that this is how it came to be named.]

The three Liver brothers were still in charge when war came again. Cecil was manager, Sidney looked after sales, and Harold was stationed in the company's Manchester office. Up to and during World War II north-western companies found it essential to be represented at the Manchester Cotton Exchange, held every Tuesday and Friday, but the Exchange's importance as a market for cotton declined when the war was ended. Harold Liver's son Jim joined up and worked his way through the ranks to become a captain in the RASC, and his daughter Nancy joined the WRNS. Sidney's son Bert was evacuated and spent his war years in Canada 6).

Mill workers joined up too, but a sufficient number remained to tend the looms, which still produced a vast range of cloths as follows:
- rayon fancies (viscose and celanese), blouse cloths (rayon), crepes, curtain cloths, dress cloths (fancy), embroideries, fancy figured cloths (rayon), gauzes, lappets (rayon), lenos (rayon), marquisettes, muslins (fancy), muslins (figured), muslins (Madras), shawls (lappet), spun fibre, voiles (fancy), rayon staple fibre fabrics 100%, also mixtures: rayon staple fibre worsted, etc. 7).

Whilst the product range had changed considerably to utilise the artificial fibres developed in the years between the wars, gauze, lappets, and muslin endured as core items.

Apart from some slight damage to the World War I memorial and adjacent property in 1941, and the arrival of a couple of searchlight units, the war years (1939-1945) passed by with little physical impact on the village. Mill hands saw their wage levels increase gradually by more than a half 8), somewhat ahead of the cost of living, and savoured their newly found entitlement to holidays with pay (introduced by government legislation in 1938). As a precautionary measure, the mill engaged firewatchers from the end of 1940 till the end of 1944, but their relevance was, fortunately, never tested 9). In 1941 one of the weaving floors introduced a night shift 10). The wartime wages ledger lists all the different jobs within the factory, which are divided into two categories. Supporting staff were on hourly pay, whereas all those whose performance directly affected production were on some kind of piece work. Weavers' pay was tied to individual output.

Tacklers' remuneration was related to factory throughput, which encouraged them to keep the looms running and in good repair. Clippers were paid by the piece, with different rates for three types of material, designated black, heavy, or light. Theirs was a specialised task requiring a keen eye, a steady hand, and a sharp knife. It was they who tidied up the lappet figuring by cutting out unwanted loops between elements of the pattern. Head shawls in current production display closely spaced figuring, so there are no surplus pattern loops, and the clippers' job has disappeared.

However, gaps between blocks of patterns occur whenever there is a border to be bridged and when one shawl ends and another begins. The corresponding loops are cut by operatives called rippers (presumably this was another part of the clipper's job in the past). The skill was to cut the loop ends close to one set of patterns, and then, holding the now loose threads with a ruler, cut the remaining strands free, again without leaving whiskers. In 1992 the job was simplified. Only one cut down the centre of the loop is required nowadays, the loose ends being sheared off by a machine to give a consistently neat finish.

The end of the war signalled change. Bert and Jim Liver returned to help with factory administration. All looms began a night shift at the end of 1946 11). A fresh boiler was installed. New weaving sheds were constructed to the east of the original structure, the ground floor emptied, and the floor above used for offices and weft preparation.

Newspaper reports from 1956 tell of the well-being of the village and the successful sales of head shawls made in Vale Mill to Iraq, Jordan, and Morocco 12). The sales record for 1956 13) paints a similar picture. Five of the three dozen customers that year accounted for half the factory output, chief amongst them being the Crown Agents for the Colonies. Similarly large orders went to two brand-new purchasers. At the other end of the scale, four companies between them bought only £59 worth of goods. In between lay that steady stream of clients, essential to every business, who turn potential loss into profit. Customer names and interests hint that much of the fabric sold to intermediaries was destined for the African and Arabian markets.

Lappets were becoming the dominant product, as confirmed by the Vale Mill entry in the 1961 Skinner's Cotton Trade Directory :
- all types of lappet fabrics in cotton, rayon, nylon, terylene, etc., including spun rayon lappets, voile lappets, and yashmaghs (the decorative head shawls worn by Muslim men).

Vale Mill had not lost the flexibility to switch production to other fabrics if need be, which became strategic when the overseas shawl trade faltered alarmingly in 1960. Some other manufacturers were not so adaptable, one such being a Glasgow firm, John Lean & Sons Ltd., established in 1840 and incorporated in 1925, of comparable age to Vale Mill. The management at Low Mill stepped in to buy them out 14), but since the shawls on order were so few (200 dozen per working week), production was sub-contracted to Vale Mill 15). Unfortunately, as recorded in chapter 9, Low Mill ceased trading in 1962. Vale Mill opened a small weaving shed on its ground floor, using some looms brought over from Low Mill. It also took the opportunity to purchase John Lean and its order book, so that it could continue to supply head shawls via an agent in Bombay. Bert Liver began a lengthy series of journeys in to the Arab world, seeking to build up personal relationships with his customers, whose means of business is always to deal with individuals (rather than corporate bodies) on a basis of mutual respect. Backed by brother Jim's inventiveness and dedication to quality, trade gradually improved, so that by the late 1960s, weekly output had risen to 500 dozen shawls 16).

When it was decided to sell Lappet to Ashton Brothers in 1964 17), Jim and Bert Liver stayed on, but Sidney opted to retire. His place as secretary was filled by Nancy, who had been attending to the office work on a part-time basis. In 1968, Courtaulds bought Ashton Brothers 18). Although both organisations added their own nominees to the board, they were content to leave day-to-day operations in the Livers' hands. Over the years this proved to be a wise decision, because, in the wake of the Arab-Israeli conflict in 1973, oil prices increased dramatically. Orders flooded in from the newly-rich Arab states, particularly from Saudi Arabia, and Bert Liver's unremitting commitment to the Middle East market began to pay handsome dividends.

After the takeover of Vale Mill in 1968, Courtaulds decided to update the factory, and increase its productivity, by replacing the traditional 'Lancashire' looms with new automatic versions. These were designed to ease the load on the operator by avoiding the need to stop the loom every time the weft in the shuttle was exhausted. Instead, the machine itself substitutes a full pirn for an empty one, quicker than the eye can see. Consequently, whereas one weaver could tend to only six looms before, they could now oversee a further ten.

A West Yorkshire loom manufacturer was consulted, and an order placed for a prototype incorporating the mechanism required to produce shawls of the superior quality normally supplied by Vale Mill. This involved the disclosure - albeit to a reputable firm - of hitherto closely guarded trade secrets. The sample proved satisfactory, and eighty looms were ordered by Lappet on the understanding that machines of this exclusive design were not to be sold to any other party.

Unhappily, some time later, the Saudi Arabian distributor advised that he had been approached by a competitor offering an identical product, and it became necessary to take the errant loom manufacturer to court for breach of confidence 19). The case was finally settled in 1981 in favour of Courtaulds. The stray loom was recovered and delivered to Vale Mill, where it has been used ever since as a training aid.

In 1979 almost every loom in the factory was producing red and white yashmaghs for Saudi Arabia, and, via the kingdom, to its neighbours, Bahrain, Kuwait, Qatar, and the United Arab Emirates. The large number of repeat orders brokered a bold decision to concentrate on this market alone. Purchase of head shawls is geared to Ramadan, a sacred period of atonement and fasting for the Muslims.

[Ramadan moves backwards in relation to the Gregorian calendar, because it is the ninth of the twelve lunar months of the Islamic year, which is approximately eleven days shorter than the Gregorian year.]

At the end of Ramadan, the Saudis celebrate *Eid Al Fitr*, which is one of the most important festivals of their year, and lasts for several days. Tradition demands that men purchase new clothes to wear during *Eid*, when it is the custom to visit friends and relatives. As a consequence, the output of head-shawls is tied in to this period, which represents an important juncture in the Vale Mill calendar, during which the previous year's sales are analysed, and plans laid for the following year's production. Other factors enter the sale calculations, including the price of oil and diplomatic relationships. Apart from the turmoil caused by the Gulf War (August 1990 to February 1991), normal fluctuations may themselves initiate a sales doldrum, as happened in January 1996, when 43 workers had to be laid off 20).

Ten years after they took over Vale Mill in 1968, Courtaulds began to plan for the day when the Livers would retire. In 1979 Brian Poole was brought in to understudy Jim Liver. He had gained much experience of weaving technology and management with the parent firm, and had previously worked for a loom manufacturer, so, when Jim decided to retire in 1985, Brian was well prepared for his promotion to Production Director.

Bob Quick, a trained accountant already supervising Vale Mill accounts as part of his financial brief with several Courtaulds units, was detailed to work full time in Calder Vale in 1984, thus allowing Nancy Liver to leave at the same time as her brother Jim. Appointed Financial Director in 1985, Bob also acted as Bert Liver's assistant on trips to the Middle East, a valuable precursor to his engagement as Managing Director when Bert retired in 1989.

This left open the post of Financial Director, filled in 1991 by Bill Hart, following a long career in textiles as a factory accountant, since 1984 with the Courtaulds group.

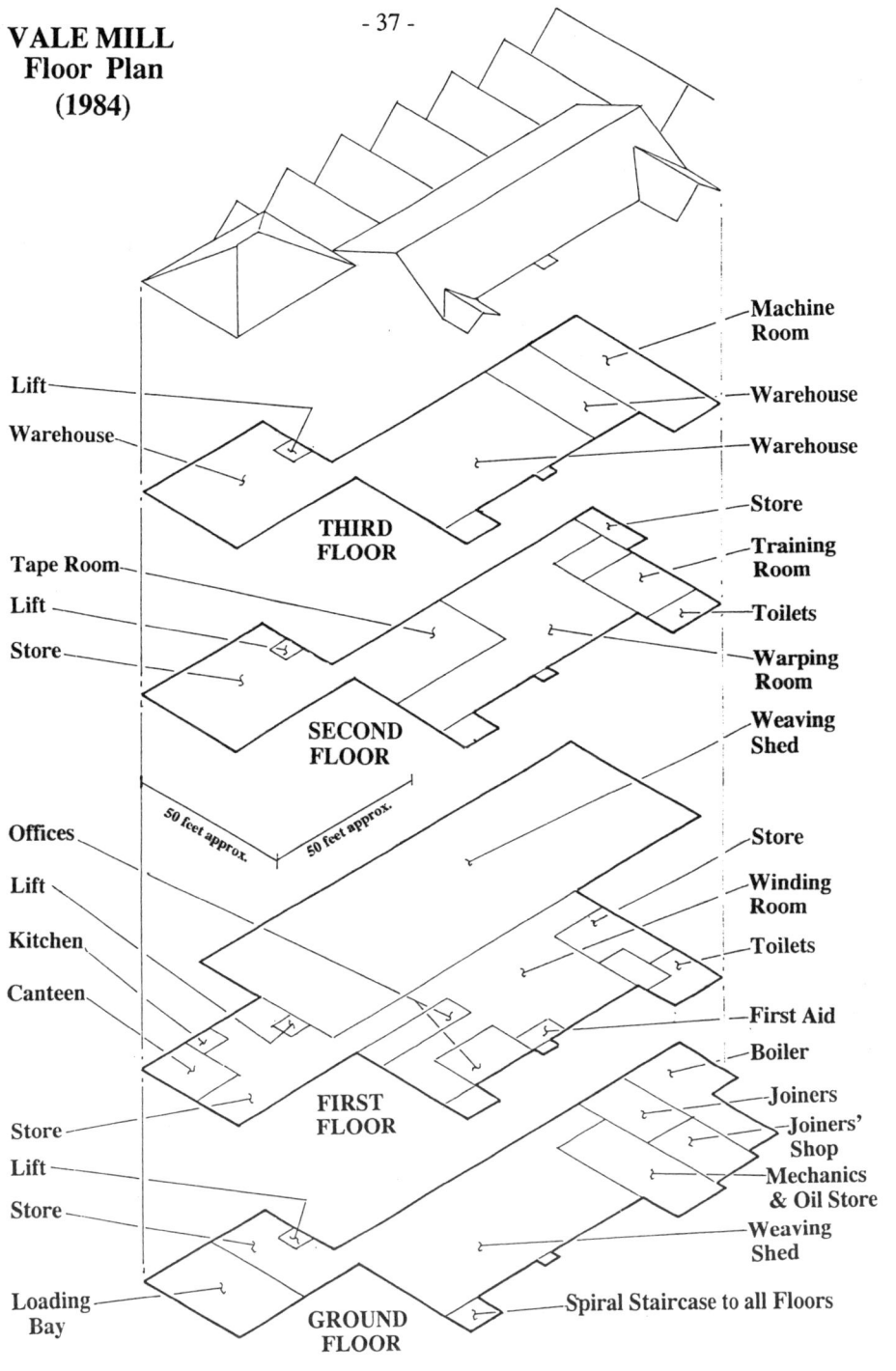

VALE MILL Floor Plan (1984)

In the meantime, Courtaulds was pursuing a process of rationalisation to bring its far flung empire under better control, culminating in the grouping of all its textile interests into one holding company - Courtaulds Textiles PLC - formed in 1990 21). Vale Mill had already experienced a symptom of this vast reorganisation in 1988, when its yarn supplies were interrupted and new arrangements had to be made. Courtaulds Textiles were of course fully aware of Vale Mill's growing order book and that its production capacity was being stretched beyond acceptable limits. Their solution to this problem is described in Chapter 8.

One weekend, in the summer of 1993, a 75 foot crane, with police escort, was cautiously steered around the sharp corner leading to the narrow access bridge leading in to mill square, edging along past the front of the mill to the south end. It had been summoned to remove and replace the ageing domed cylindrical boiler, but first it had to lift off the boiler house roof to gain access. 'The Beast', as it had come to be known, had been salvaged from a sunken ship in Glasson Dock in 1949, and had served Vale Mill well for the intervening forty-four years. However, it was becoming increasingly difficult for this boiler to meet its annual pressure check requirement. Its replacement was a functional metal box, devoid of outward grace, but bristling with all the latest electronic control gear. Out came the old, in went the new, the roof was refitted, the crane and the Beast, now strapped to an articulated lorry, renegotiated the difficult exit bend, and Monday's shift began work almost as though nothing had happened, except that yet another link with the past had been severed. On a lighter note, also in 1993, one Friday noon at the end of April, Brian Poole made a noble sacrifice 22). The beard he had treasured for the past twenty-six years was shaved away in front of a large audience, raising the goodly sum of £1000 for childrens' charities from donations by both employees and suppliers.

In 1996, Courtaulds Textiles sold Vale Mill, having decided that it no longer fitted within its core business plan 23). All the Lappet premises (including the satellites) were handed over, together with all the management and staff, and everything left unchanged by the new owners.

8. Lappet Satellites

Lappet is now supported by three satellites, all of which were conceived about the time of the Gulf War, and initiated by Courtaulds Textiles as part of their consolidation programme.

The first satellite to be fully operational was purpose built, with money allocated by Courtaulds to compensate for their closure, in 1988, of the previous dyed yarn supplier, although they kept a small section open until the new facilities came on stream. Construction in Lancaster commenced in 1989 at a cost of just over £1 million, and the Dye House was officially opened in May 1990. The dyeing process, whilst not altogether exclusive, is one favoured by Lappet to give a pronounced brightness and permanence to the tinted yarn.

The plant was designed to match the pace of Lappet production, but it has the capacity to take in work from outside when the need arises. For example, in 1995, a batch was processed for British Airways, who had a specific requirement for coloured thread capable of withstanding a flame proofing treatment, which could not be met by other dye-houses.

The next necessity was to expand the weaving potential, which meant finding more floor space in another mill. Originally a factory near Skipton was thought to be ideal, but administrative delays provoked by the Gulf War ruled out this option. Alternatives were explored elsewhere within the Courtaulds group, and the most suitable prospect was an empty half of a weaving factory in Carlisle which was producing cloth for car seats. Operation commenced in late 1990, inside an empty shell equipped with twenty-four brand new looms which had been modified using local engineering expertise controlled directly by Lappet. Members of Calder Vale's skilled staff travelled by coach each day over a period to instruct locally recruited employees. As demand has grown, the site has expanded, and today output almost matches that of Vale Mill.

The third satellite grew from customer demand for fancy hemming (in the style of hand-crafted drawn thread work). Enquiries around the extensive Courtaulds facilities revealed that a factory in Clitheroe would soon become surplus to requirement, and speedy arrangements were made to transfer it to Lappet along with the majority of its workforce in March 1991. Goods from the weaving sheds are routed to Clitheroe via an independent finishing factory for hemming, brand stamping, and packing.

The Clitheroe hemming factory is located in what was once the Mount Zion Methodist church, featured in a 'matchstick people' painting by L. S. Lowry. It has been a factory for about fifty years : originally Searsons, making school uniforms, then Jacobs (who sold it to Courtaulds some twenty-five years ago), Granby Garments, Elgin, and then back to Granby Garments making underwear, nightwear, and swimwear. At the time of transfer to Lappet, it was making underwear for Marks & Spencer.

The opening of satellites at Lancaster and Clitheroe gave Lappet an opportunity to introduce a multi-skilling policy wherever feasible, which offers advantages to both management and staff, and has since been implemented at all sites. In case of a sudden surge in demand, people can be moved from one job to another to concentrate on the most urgent tasks. At times of exceptional absenteeism, jobs can be switched around to avoid production disruption. The workforce benefits because they are not confined to one activity all the time, and gains satisfaction by wider involvement and experience within the company.

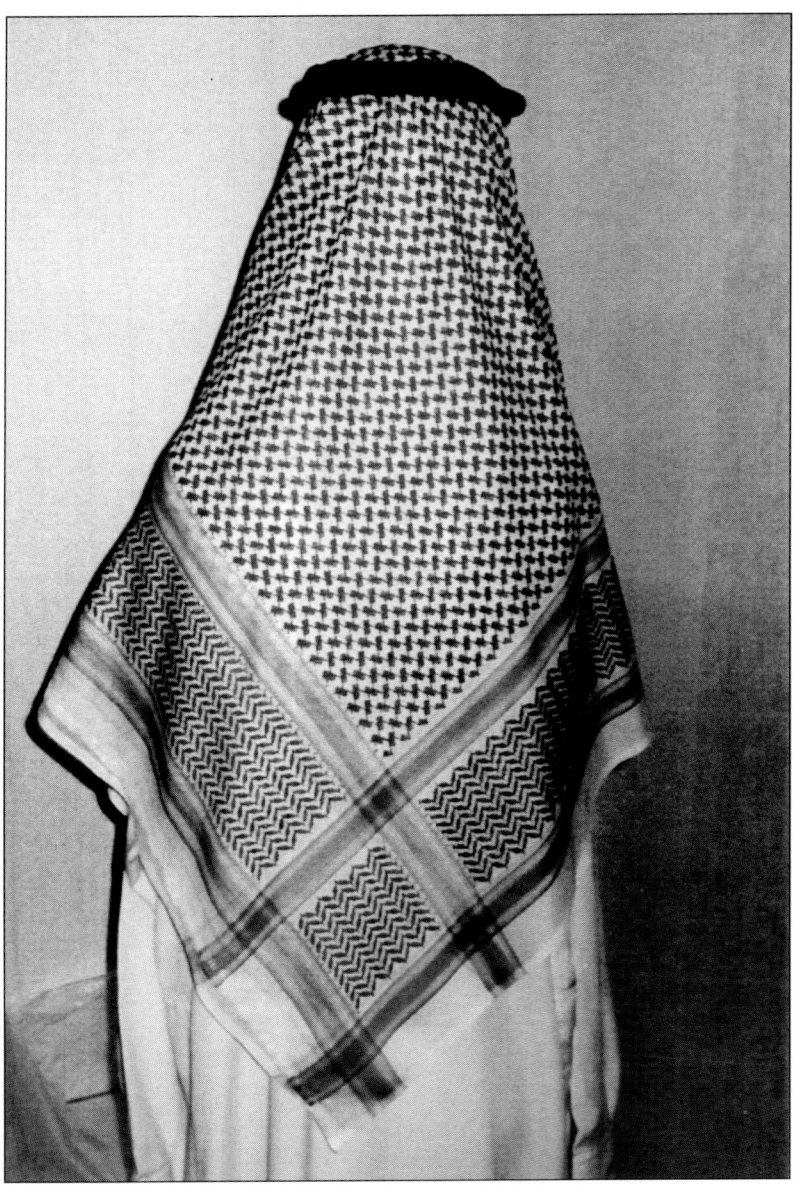

i. The red and white Lappet Headshawl in current production

ii. James W. Whitehead
who purchased Low Mill in 1909

iii. **Humphrey Whitehead**
Son of James

iv. Arthur Whitehead (1884 - 1930)

v. Fred Whitehead (1878 - 1956)

vi. Barnacre and Grisedale Reservoirs

vii. Inside the Barnacre Filter House

viii. Aerial view of Oakenclough paper mill prior to expansion

ix. Aerial view of the 'Bag Factory'

x. 1964: The Beloit-Walmsley 120 inch paper machine

xi. 1970: Oakenclough Paper Mill
Presentation of long service awards

xii. David Jackson

9. Low Mill *See page 45 for site plan*

To resume the story of Low Mill, following the death of Jonathan Jackson in 1886, a bleak midwinter of stalled production descended on Calder Vale, extending well beyond the normal Christmas season. With no cotton mill to provide a wage, no state aid, only limited charity, and meagre handouts to those wise enough to have become members of a friendly society, times were hard. Nevertheless, the majority of villagers stayed put, hoping for the tide to turn. More than six months elapsed before a purchaser for Low Mill came forward. In April 1887 a Blackburn company announced its intention to fill the factory with 290 new looms, to be driven by combined steam and water power 1). Purchase was completed in June, and a new boiler and engine installed 2).

The 1891 census returns identify 108 cotton mill workers, including a manager and four overlookers, so that, for every pair of houses, there were three workers. Every weaver (two thirds of them female) looked after four looms. It could be claimed that Low Mill had saved the village, but it was not all plain sailing. In December 1890 workers withdrew their labour for three days to protest about the quality of material supplied and the wages paid 3), and again, in May 1894, half the '90 persons ... employed at the mill' went on strike for a week 4).

In 1891 the Fylde Waterworks Company, having already purchased Vale Mill in anticipation of a favourable outcome, petitioned Parliament to allow diversion of water from the Calder river. Low Mill stood alone in objection, claiming a need for water to drive their machinery. However, when the bill received its Royal Assent, the only water Low Mill was allowed was for its steam engine, as much as could be taken through a six inch inside diameter pipe. The water wheel had been deprived of its sustenance, had been given notice of retirement, and would have to be dismantled.

Towards the end of the year, the Water Company began negotiations to buy the mill, and brought in an arbitrator to agree the price, who crystallised the sale at £8102.12s.6d. in September 1892 5). This deal was to usher in a few years of uncertainty for the village and its inhabitants.

The Water Company had gained indisputable control over the river water, but, in return, was saddled with irksome ownership responsibilities outside its remit. In September 1893 the directors decided to advertise the whole of their property in Calder Vale, exclusive of water rights, for sale or to let 6).

Records for the next few years confuse the issue of ownership and use. In 1895, Mr. Liver's name crops up during negotiations as the Water Company sought to dispose of its various Calder Vale properties, and the journalist Anthony Hewitson, in his book *Northward*, confirmed the utilisation of Low Mill in 1900 when he wrote 'The shed is worked by Messrs. Liver and Co., who purchased it from the Waterworks Company', however, the Barnacre-with-Bonds valuation lists 7) present an intermix of interested parties as follows:

Date	Owner	Occupier
1896	Albert Mill Co	J.W.Liver & Co
1897	Albert Mill Co	Albert Mill Co
1898	Albert Mill Co	J.W.Liver & Co
1901	Barnacre Weaving Co + J.W.Liver	J.W.Liver & Co
1908	J.W.Liver	J.W.Liver

(The Barnacre Weaving Company, incorporated on 31.7.1895, operated from Albert Mill in Preston, with Mr James Whitehead as secretary).

These same partners crop up in a sales ledger 8) spanning the period from Spring 1898 to 1902. Amongst the 78 firms catalogued are major entries for James W Liver (at both Kent Street Mill in Preston and at the mill in Calder Vale) and the Barnacre Weaving Company at Albert Mill, Preston. Another page recognises some kind of Barnacre Weaving Company presence in Calder Vale. Here is strong evidence of prior collaboration between a seller and his eventual buyer.

Incidentally, this same ledger includes several transactions with the National Telephone Company, a reminder that telephone links with Calder Vale and Oakenclough had been forged only months beforehand, in 1897 9).

On 17.6.1909, the 'Calder Vale Weaving Shed (owned by the Barnacre Weaving Co Ltd)' and an associated 37 cottages were put up for auction 10). The factory buildings comprised the following : weaving shed, warehouse, winding room, warping room, heald store room, tape room, size mixing room, boiler house, engine house, watch house, and offices. Machinery included a steam boiler, a horizontal compound steam engine, a 150 horse-power turbine, 316 looms (260 fitted with dobbies and most of which had lappet motions), and various other machines essential to the task. Both gas and electric lighting was installed. Barnacre House was also included in the sale.

Valuation Lists 11) were slow to recognise the change of ownership, showing the 'Calder Vale Manufacturing Company' as owner / occupier from 1915, and belatedly recognising J W Whitehead as owner / occupier in 1920. Local directories listed the Barnacre Weaving Company as operational at Low Mill from 1910 onwards. Whatever the title of the company, it is certain that James W Whitehead ('a fair man, but a hard man') arrived after the sale to reside at Barnacre House, and to manage his new acquisition in Calder Vale, in addition to his Preston factory, assisted by his younger brothers, Fred and Arthur. Fred acted as secretary. Arthur, the youngest, looked after the commercial interests, his career interrupted by World War I when he joined the South Lancashire Regiment 12). In 1914, 1200 square yards of floorspace were added to the weaving sheds 13), and cotton trade directories confirm that 318 looms were in use at the end of the war. In 1924, the warping room was increased by 75 sq. yd. 14).

The 1929 Wall Street crash launched an economic crisis in world trade, a run on the pound, and increased unemployment, seriously affecting the cotton industry. Albert Mill in Preston ceased trading. James steered Low Mill through the doldrums, despite losing Arthur to pneumonia in 1930 (aged only 46), and suffering the resignation of Fred soon afterwards 15).

The entry for the Barnacre Weaving Company in Skinner's Cotton Trade Directory for 1940/41 was far from gloomy. The Manchester office was still in being. One-hundred-and-fifty employees and 318 looms were producing cloths up to 56 inches wide. James' son, Humphrey, had become the general manager and salesman 16), with an extensive range of fabrics on offer. These included : cellulars, checks, crepes, curtain cloths, Doria stripes, embroideries, fancy figured cloths, lappets, lawns (figured), lenos, marquisettes, mercerised cotton fancies, muslins (figured), organdies (figured), voiles (fancy), and rayon staple fibre yarns used in combination with cotton.

In 1949, Humphrey decided to retire to the Isle of Man, where he had been educated as a young man, and sold out to Vivian Hill. Management continuity over the changeover period was provided by Tom Ward (company secretary) and senior staff employees 17). Under the new direction numbers were reduced : looms to 220, employees to one hundred, and the product range restricted. Lappet designs were woven on to plain, dobby, Dorian and leno grounds in grey, coloured and rayon lappet 18).

Journalists came to view the village in 1956 19). They were much surprised to learn from Mr. Smeddle, one of the directors, that 80% of the factory output was destined for export to countries around the world, including Scandinavia, Africa, the Americas, and the antipodes. The works manager, Bill Craig, took them through the factory to see designs being transferred from paper to the laminated wheels used to juggle the loom mechanism into adding pattern to the weave. Previous visits to weaving sheds, in other places, had conditioned the guests to expect sight of still more monotonous rows of clattering looms, producing identical miles of plain white cotton sheeting. Their expectation was to be confounded. As shuttles sped and needles pranced around the shimmering warp threads, design and colour appeared like magic, providing them with a 'wonderful display', and a better appreciation for the skill and dignity of this sequestered workforce.

LOW MILL
Site Plan

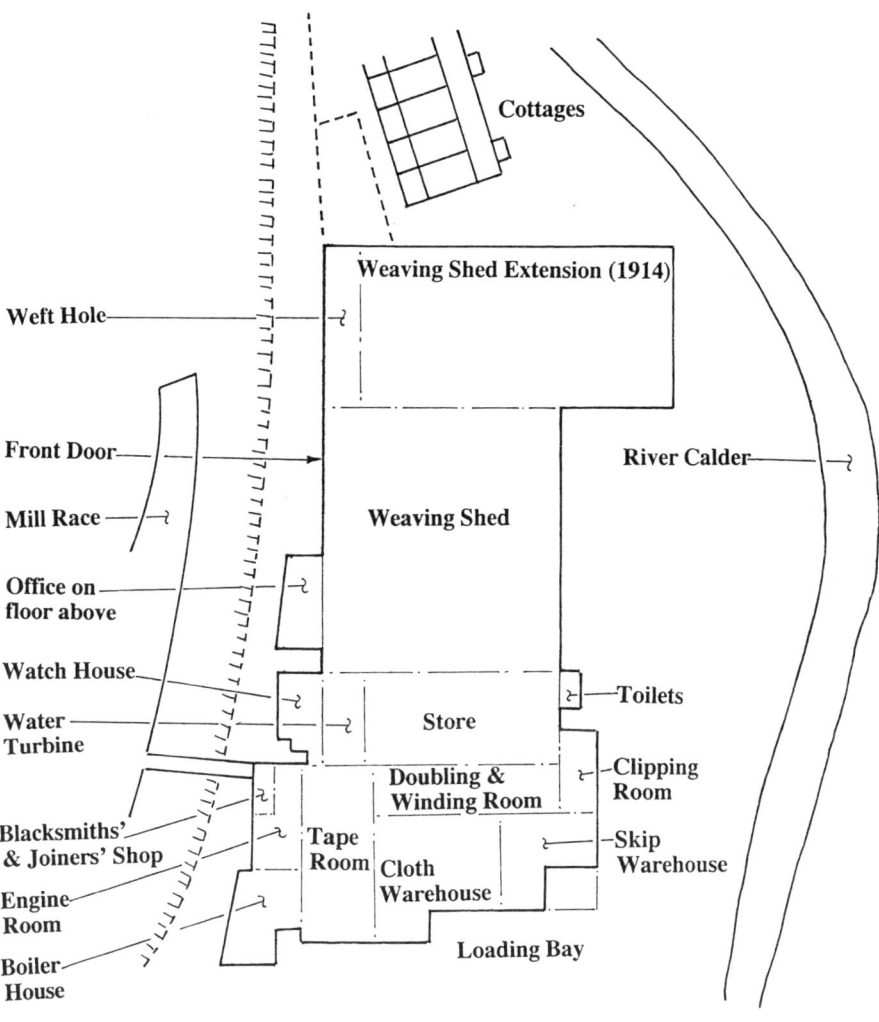

Outline : taken from LRO/RDG 19/1/1914/48
Internal Layout :
as remembered by former employee Tom Jennings

In 1962, news gatherers came again 20), this time to deplore the passing of Low Mill. Bill Craig, over forty years an employee, was there once more to greet them, along with others who had worked there since their schooldays, but on this occasion there was no happy tale to tell. Looms had been reduced to 130, employees to sixty or seventy, and already machinery was being dismantled, with a view to closure in July.

Upstream, production was booming in the paper mill at Oakenclough, with every nook and cranny occupied with manufacture. Storage space was at a premium. Apart from the need to conserve machinery and spare parts, an embarrassing problem arose at every product change by the creation of a mass of combustible start-up waste, which could be recycled, but needed to be kept somewhere in the meantime. The empty premises at Low Mill offered a convenient resting place 21).

With the closure of the paper mill in 1971, Low Mill lost its reprieve. The physical remains were dismantled and taken away; its spirit consigned to the hearts and minds of that loyal band of villagers who, over so many fruitful years, had given it creative life and from whence, in fair exchange, they had gleaned their livelihood.

Part 2

Paper

Dates of Relevance

1670 Hollander Beater introduced about this time
1775 Oakenclough paper mill began trading
1801 Thomas Curtis died, leaving Oakenclough paper mill to his son Richard
1806 Paper making machine patented by Fourdrinier brothers
1826 Richard Curtis declared bankrupt
1827 John Jackson purchased Oakenclough paper mill
1840 Garstang and Catterall railway station opened
1845 John Jackson died, leaving the paper mill to his sons Richard and James
1861 Paper tax abolished
1862 Agreement signed to use esparto grass as raw material at Oakenclough
1864 Oakenclough paper mill lit by gas
1889 Richard Jackson died
1890 James Jackson died, leaving the paper mill to his son Harold
1893 Contract placed to build a 'Bag factory' next to G & C railway station
1900 Oakenclough paper mill water wheel replaced by other means
1946 Mains electricity wired to Oakenclough as a whole
1947 Harold Jackson died, leaving the paper mill to his sons 'Hal' and 'Will'
1954 Inveresk Paper Company bought Oakenclough paper mill
1954 'Hal' Jackson retired
1957 Major expansion of paper mill completed
1962 'Bag factory' expanded by construction of new premises
1962 Further expansion of paper mill,
      including installation of 120 inch Beloit-Walmsley machine
1966 Piped water fed to Oakenclough
1967 Paper mill merged with British Tissues
1968 'Will' Jackson retired, handing over to his son David
1969 Garstang and Catterall railway station closed
1971 Oakenclough paper mill ceased trading

10. Paper Making

All advanced manufacturing processes can trace their origins to simple beginnings, and paper is no exception. In AD 105, Tsai Lun, a Chinese court official, shredded some old fishing nets and rags, mixed them with fragmented hemp and mulberry bark, and steeped the resulting combination in water. He carefully spread the pulp evenly on to a sieve, allowed it first to drain and then to dry out completely. By these means he was able to achieve a surface smooth enough to be used for writing. His technique remains valid today for the individual craftsman who wishes to produce distinctive papers in small quantities, and who can afford to work without regard to the binding restraints of time or economy.

It is generally accepted that the West did not become acquainted with the art of paper making until the eighth century, when Chinese families came to practice their craft in Turkey. The oldest surviving piece of paper to be found in the Public Record Office dates back to 1220, but it was not until Tudor times that paper began to overtake the use of parchment as a recording medium. The development of the printing press in fifteenth-century Europe, by such pioneers as Johannes Gutenberg (c.1400-1468) in Mainz in Germany and William Caxton (c.1492-c.1491) in England, stimulated the demand for writing material and justified the establishment of factories to produce stock of the necessary quality and quantity, and encouraged the design of inventions intended to improve productivity. A major innovation was the Hollander beater (commonly referred to as the 'engine' by paper makers), introduced about 1670, which enabled rags (the principal raw material at the time) to be shredded and pulped by rotary motion instead of pummelling by hammer action. However, centuries old routines persisted for the remaining processes, and it was not until about 1800 that attempts were made to form sheets of paper by mechanical methods.

By 1807 sufficient development had been made to promise commercial success to a machine ascribed to two English brothers, Henry and Sealy Fourdrinier, which was capable of taking in pulped raw material at one end and transforming it at the other into a continuous roll of paper.

Modern programmes, for all their sophistication, follow the same route to realisation : the selection of ingredients, their cleaning and homogenisation, their suspension in liquid form, followed by consistent transfer to some form of draining device, and a final drying out and finishing process. The difficulties encountered at each stage, which involved many years of design and experimentation to reach a satisfactory solution, can be envisaged by closer consideration of the craft methods employed prior to the mechanisation of the industry.

Raw materials were chosen for their suitability, cost and ready availability. Second hand materials such as rags and ropes had to be sorted and chopped, and dirt and bark and pith extracted from wood and grass and the like. Cleanliness was a priority to be achieved by mechanical means and thorough washing. The next process was to reduce the chosen blend to small short fibres by stamping or beating. This was done by water driven hammers, prior to the introduction of the Hollander beater. The resulting mix was placed in liquid suspension in a vat.

The skill of the vatman, who stirred the pulp with a paddle, spooned some out into one side of his straining mould and tipped it back and forth to control the thickness, and finally gave it a shake to lock the fibres together, needed to be transfigured into continuous motion, and this proved to be a major hurdle. Working in close cooperation with the vatman was the coucher, whose job was to transfer the wet sheet of paper from the mould to a piece of damp felt. His task was to build up a pile of alternate layers of paper and felt, ready for squeezing in a large screw press, when it was customary for other workers to be called in so that maximum leverage could be applied. On removal, a third member of the team, the layer, separated the sheets of paper from the felts. It could take literally all day for the three of them to produce four thousand sheets of paper : a laudable effort then, but minuscule in relation to today's machine-aided output. The pack of still damp sheets was taken to the top of the building to be hung over ropes to dry. The dried sheets were taken down, sized, hung again, and finally brought down for smoothing before despatch to the customer.

After much trial and error, mechanical techniques were established which translated these stepped manual operations into one continuous process, epitomised in the Fourdrinier patent of 1806. An even film of slush was spread evenly on to a moving belt of finely woven wire mesh, which was jostled to interlock the fibres. The bulk of the water drained away through the interstices before the pulp was swallowed between pairs of press rollers covered in felt. Emerging from these, the paper had to be dry enough to be transferred from the moving wire onto a 'couch roller'. Size could have been applied at this stage or later as the sheet advanced through or over a succession of cylinders to complete the drying process. Smoothing, glazing, slitting, and cutting would follow, according to the customer's requirements. Condensing this whole process to a few words gives a simplistic view of what is actually quite an elaborate proceeding.

Paper making machines tie up a great deal of capital and occupy a lot of floor space, so it is necessary that they work at high speed and be kept busy. Where a mill produces a variety of products, which may be thick or thin, plain or crinkled, and made from recipes using different raw materials, then it must be possible to change from one product to another with the minimum of upset and delay. The machinery must be well designed, and every part finely tuned to ensure the creation of a quality end result. The pulp must be homogeneous with no lumps or impurities, it must spread evenly and consistently across the width of the wire belt with no build up at sides or centre, the correct amount of water must be extracted at each stage, the rollers must revolve in sympathy to avoid stretching or creasing, and the sizing, drying and finishing operations must all be closely controlled.

Add to all this the complication of making many and different special purpose products on one or other machine, as came to be the case at Oakenclough, and the need to assemble and retain a skilled and adaptable workforce becomes self evident.

11. Oakenclough Paper Mill   *See pages 57 and 63 for site layouts*

In 1775, when the Oakenclough paper mill started to trade, the British paper-making industry was expanding (345 Excise licences were issued that year), and rags (a major raw material at the time) were having to be imported from abroad.

Confirmed as owner of Oakenclough paper mill in the Bleasdale Land Tax returns for 1785, Thomas Curtis, yeoman, retained ownership until his death in 1801. He left his land and 'one Paper-mill and its appurtinances' to his eldest son Richard. However, the luckless Richard, 'paper manufacturer', was declared bankrupt on 15 September 1826. As a consequence, John Jackson, farming adjoining land, was able to buy the mill in November 1827 for the sum of £2990 1).

Jackson realised that his acquisition would pay dividends only if he were to expand the business, so he secured land, previously part of adjacent Calder Mouth farm, in order to enlarge the mill pond to drive the large water wheel needed to power new machinery. Stock records and operating statistics for 1832 indicate an average daily production of four hundredweights of paper, confirming a requirement for several engines. The purchase of wires and felt in the same year 2) also implies the existence of a Fourdrinier, although this did not altogether usurp hand crafting, which was employed as an alternative method of production throughout the nineteenth century.

The majority of John Jackson's customers and suppliers lay within a twelve-mile radius 3), which represented a daily outward and return limit for horse-drawn waggons traversing rural by-ways. Rope from Glasson Dock was converted into coarse wrapping papers; mill and flax waste, and rags, also obtained from nearby sources, were transformed into fine quality bag papers intended for tea and other refined products. Amongst the nine employees designated as paper makers in Oakenclough in the 1841 census, one is specifically listed as a 'rag chopper'. His job was to slice pieces of cloth into four inch squares and sort the resulting scraps into categories. Seams and stitching were separated out, since they required extra beating.

Serving customers further away entailed one or more overnight stops using waggons drawn by teams of horses. The passage to London took ten days, so arrangements were negotiated to ease the burden of travel by exchanging loads in Derby with firms in the capital plying their trade in Lancashire 4). The goods remained in transit for ten days just the same, but the carter arrived back for his next load that much sooner. In 1840, nearby railtrack was completed and a station opened three miles to the south-west to serve the Garstang and Catterall district. Road access from the paper mill in that direction was hindered by a steep rise from the valley, so John Jackson created a less demanding by-pass road through neighbouring farm land, which he donated to the highway authorities 5). Expansion into a wider market thus eased, deliveries throughout Lancashire and into neighbouring counties became much more feasible, and are included in an 1849 goods consignment book.

In 1845, Jackson, in his mid-fifties, died quite suddenly. His sons, Richard and James, were still in their early teens, so, until they were twenty-five, other family members, named as executors, were instructed by John's will to continue the business and provide relevant statistics every six months. Good records of production had to be maintained anyway, because all paper produced before 1861 was subject to taxation (in 1836 the rate was three halfpence per pound weight). The accounts confirm substantial sales (£12 186 annually in 1851 as compared with £1152 for six months in 1832) and imply that new machinery was financed directly from profits, since no interest payments on loans to purchase equipment are logged. A Sun Insurance policy dated 1847 includes a 'New Water-Wheel House' ... a 'New Warehouse' and an 'Old Rag Engine House'. A simultaneous allusion to a 'Steam Engine and Boiler House' suggests that a major refurbishment had just been completed.

Most of the mid-century output consisted of various types of wrapping paper destined for the domestic retail trade. Point-of-sale facilities were becoming more organised to cope with an increased flow of commodities, and traders were feeling the need to envelop and protect their wares for the purchasers' journeys home.

Grocers and tea dealers were particularly good customers, and as the number of co-operative societies multiplied, following the success of the Rochdale Pioneers in 1844, orders from this source began to predominate. Whilst a skilled purveyor, without staple or glue, could transform a paper sheet into a robust container with a few deft folds and tucks, the paper sales inventory nevertheless expanded to include an additional and rising demand for ready-made time-saving paper bags.

Rags were becoming scarcer and dearer as Richard and James took up their inheritance in 1855/1857 and so were compelled to pursue alternatives. Following their father's example, they were quick to sign a ten-year agreement with Thomas Routledge in 1862 to purchase and process esparto grass in accordance with his method, patented only two years beforehand 6). Also about this time a high pressure steam engine was installed, a second Fourdrinier machine brought into operation, and gas lighting introduced (in 1864). Later records confirm further investments under the direction of Richard and James Jackson in the form of paper machine alterations, a rag engine and boiler, and a third Fourdrinier, perhaps as a replacement for the first one.

Census returns provide useful details about the size and skill of the workforce as each decade passed by from 1841 to 1891. A tabulation of the Oakenclough schedule can be found in Appendix D. There is an unfortunate inconsistency in job description, with some tasks masquerading as an ubiquitous 'paper maker', and it is possible that other operatives are concealed under some other description : an 1885 payroll lists thirty-two mill workers in comparison with the 1881/1891 census figures of twenty-one and twenty-five employees respectively. The terms 'willow tenter' (a ten-year-old boy employed to operate an internally spiked cleansing machine in 1851) and 'mindsa scutcher' (beaterman) would have confounded the enumerator. However, clear trends are apparent, like the increased use of female labour as the century progresses, and the introduction of office staff in 1881. The importation of knowledge is implied by workers from some distance away appearing once only in the decadic schedules.

When Richard Jackson died in 1889, followed by James in 1890, the wrapping paper business was in decline. James' son, Harold, almost twenty-five years old, was soon to take over and bring into play his ripening innovative skills.

A threat to the water supply came about in 1891 when the Fylde Waterworks Company petitioned Parliament to take water from the River Calder 7). No doubt an idea to dam Nanny Brook, a tributary joining the Calder at the paper mill, would have entered into discussion at this time, for the stream could then also have been used to replenish the mill lodge. Albert Simpson, Harold's uncle by marriage, was uniquely placed to effect the necessary liaison with the reservoir management. Not only was he an executor and director of the paper mill; he was also a director (and later chairman) of the water company.

During the House of Lords examination of the Fylde Waterworks Company submission, it became evident that the paper mill discharges were seriously polluting the Calder, and that discarded ashes and cinders had been allowed to accumulate in Nanny Brook. Although under no obligation to do so, but thereby facilitating the passage of the Bill, the Water Company volunteered 'to filter the outcast from the Oakenclough paper works and make their discharge to that extent innocuous to the river' 8).

Bags for grocers' dry goods had been produced by hand labour throughout the Jackson stewardship (see Appendix D). The Bleasdale 1891 census includes twelve reformatory boys described as paper bag makers. One way to fortify the business was to automate this part of the operation and expand into other finishing and packaging processes, thereby reducing Oakenclough's dependence on middlemen. This Harold Jackson did, in 1893, by engaging Richard Hall, of Forton, to build a conversion plant ('the bag factory') near to Garstang and Catterall railway station, alongside the Preston to Kendal canal 9). Positioning the building so close to transport facilities partially eased the problems caused by the geographic position of the paper mill, isolated as it was by rough country roads, which were, and even today are, occasionally rendered impassable in the worst of winter weather.

Engineering works (by Dryden of Preston) continued apace at Oakenclough. A Yates and Thom steam engine, costing £900, was installed in 1892 10).

Between Nanny Brook and the mill lodge lay eight acres of land which Harold Jackson, who had a passion for things piscatorial, transformed into a breeding ground for trout and salmon. Fry ponds and plant ponds alternated, with a fall between each to aerate the pure spring water. A dam had been built across Nanny Brook to supplement the water supply to the mill, creating a small lake to the rear of Calder Bank, the Jackson family home, which could accommodate the largest fish if the need arose. After a few experimental years, the fishery had become a successful business in its own right by 1902, incubating a million eggs annually 11).

A 1912 plan (see facing page) and inventory exist to pinpoint the various buildings and equipments in use prior to World War I. Two of the four 3.5 cwt. beaters were of 'Jackson's Patent' design, and a 'Jackson's Refiner' was in use. The two paper machines were producing sheets 60 inches wide, and a 70 horse power Gilkes water turbine had replaced the water wheel. An experimental room above the pump and gearing house contained an 'experimental beater or grinder, sample rag boiler, sample beater and grinder', all confirming an ongoing search for new ideas and techniques to keep Oakenclough at the leading edge of development.

Apart from the introduction of new concepts, it was becoming evident that greater output was needed than the two 60 inch machines could provide. Even though they worked slowly compared with later models, one was retained for the manufacture of specialities. The other was replaced with an 80 inch machine which could produce towelling and kraft papers at a much faster rate. Each additional or bigger machine demanded more power, so, about 1930, power lines were brought to the mill so that electricity could be imported from Preston power station.

Oakenclough Paper Mill
Use of Buildings : 1912

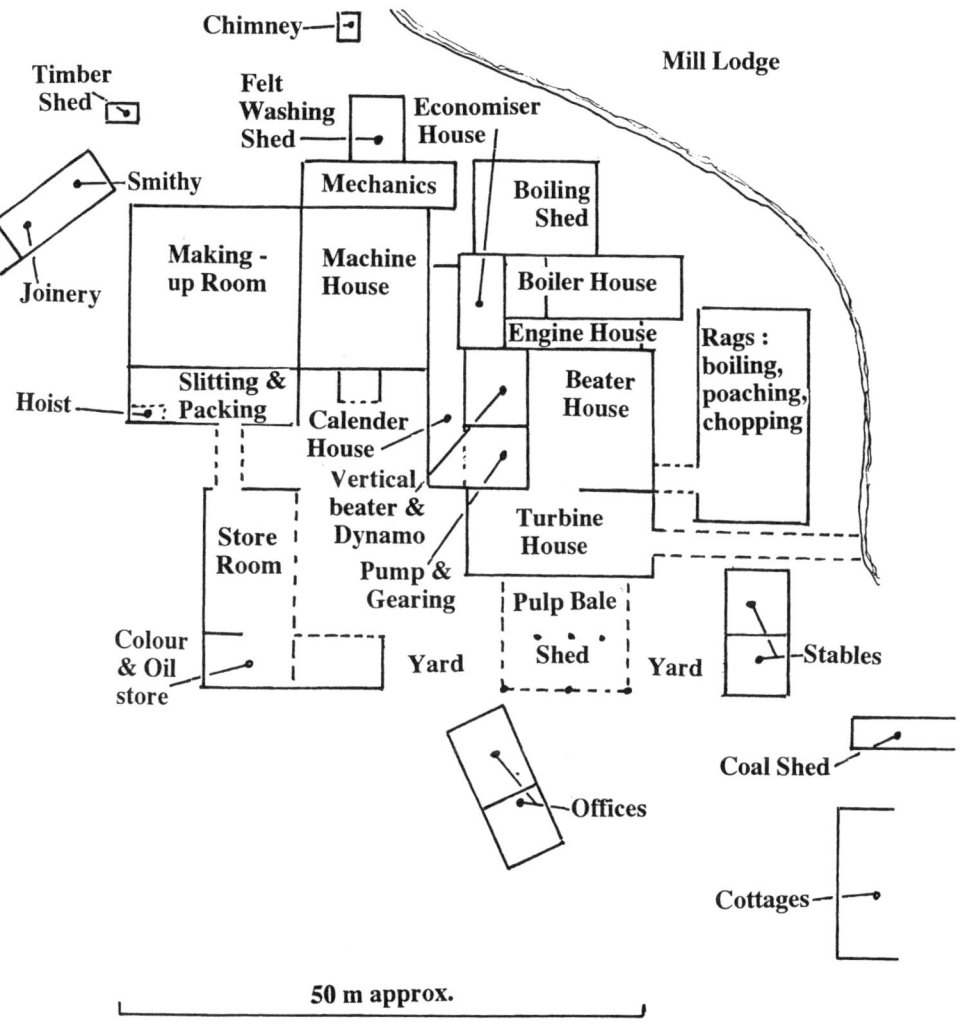

New lines merited trade names. One of the earliest was *Oaklin* for paper towels. A pictorial trademark was registered in the punning form of oak leaves and acorns, and printed on relevant products or their wrappers as an earnest of their authenticity from Oakenclough.

Long before the mass market for paper towelling came into being, Harold was experimenting to find an ideal balance between wet strength and the absorbency appropriate to such a product. Having succeeded, he looked around for a market, and, by the 1920s, was exporting huge quantities of his *Oaklin* towels, in packs of 150, to Argentina.

The names *Oakenstrong* and *Oakencork* were coined later to brand the oil resistant gasket materials used for many years in automotive applications.

Whilst Harold Jackson's major preoccupation was to manage the mill, this was by no means his only concern. He retained a strong interest in the farm (run by his brother John James), pioneering and nurturing a national milk recording scheme 12). The local community benefited from his activities as J.P., tax commissioner, and district councillor. For relaxation, he busied himself with his fishery, photography, and crosswords.

Sample books, covering a few individual years between 1890 and 1940, held by the Lancashire Record Office 13), display the range of products evolved under his direction to meet the demands of a changing market. Representative of the many and varied ingredients used in their manufacture were cotton clips, manilla, noils and scotch tow to provide the fibrous content; gypsum and china clay as fillers; alum, wax, or glue as binding agents; and a spectrum of dyes in every combination of primary colours from palest pink to carbon black. The samples, all dated and annotated with recipes, provide an indication of when new types of paper were introduced, and whether or not they stayed the course. The table on the next page presents a summary.

Year	New and repeated later	Single year mention
1897	Kraft, Cookery	Sanitary
1905	Cartridge, Crinkled	Asbestos, Black photo album
1908	Insulating	Woollen
1914	Chemical	
1920	Towels	
1924	Filter, Linen, *Oakenstrong*	Emery base
1932/4	*Velvoride*, Jointing	Cement bag, Hair curling
1939/40	*Oakencork, Palmolive*	Vacuum bag

Paper can be crinkled by means of a delicately adjusted 'doctor knife' which pares the slightly moist, partly adhering sheet from its drying cylinder, causing it to pucker in the required manner. At Oakenclough a technique was developed whereby striations were induced as the paper ran between the press rollers after leaving the couch rollers, before it reached the final drying cylinder. Crinkled paper, with its built-in stretch, is quite versatile. White crinkle was used to filter edible oils in margarine manufacture; blue crinkle interlined hessian sacks carrying sugar; two inch wide strips of brown crinkle were sewn across the ends of cement sacks. At one time seven-ton loads of brown crinkle strip were being despatched weekly to the Portland cement works.

Two sample books contain rather less variety than the others. The 1908 collection is dominated by orders from the Co-operative Wholesale Society (CWS), who that year bought a great deal of wrapping paper from the mill. In 1940 the thirty-seven men and fourteen women employed at Oakenclough spent most of their workdays producing green crinkled paper and *Velvoride*, a hardy leather substitute. The former was used to wrap tablets of the popular *Palmolive* toilet soap; the latter product had been exported to Germany before World War II for use in the manufacture of luggage, belts and shoes, but was now serving similar purposes closer to home.

Joan Haines, a niece by marriage, remembers visiting her uncle Harold many times in his upstairs office overlooking the entrance yard. On one occasion he extracted a sample of *Velvoride* from his shoe, where the tough fabric was being submitted to an ad hoc wearability test. 'Try to tear this', he suggested, with a twinkle in his eye, knowing full well she would find it impossible. During the search for further suitable applications, one of his trials had been to upholster son Hal's car seats in dashing red *Velvoride*.

In 1947 Harold Jackson died, but by this time his two sons, brought up in the business, were well positioned to assume his place at the helm. Young Harold (Hal) returned from National Service and took control of sales. William (Will) looked after manufacture, having remained at the mill throughout the war years to oversee the production of the strategic gasket and jointing materials.

The family enterprise had suffered twice within fifteen years because of death duties. When John James died in 1932 the farm had been surrendered. Harold Jackson's death scuppered imminent plans for expansion, and encouraged his heirs to seek some kind of haven. In 1954 the Inveresk Paper Company stepped in to buy up the shares 14), and provided money to add machinery and extend the site. Hal retired, but Will stayed on as managing director. The first physical evidence of the new investment came to Garstang Rural District Council's attention in December 1955, when earth removal began and the mill was reminded that such action needed council permission 15).

Planning applications were submitted and agreed during the following twelve months 16), taking into use almost all the land available between the mill lodge and the river. First of all came the tip extension, followed in succession by a weir, a hydrapulper building, a large machine house straddling the river, a lavatory block, a power plant, and a repositioned chimney, 140 feet tall.

The energy needed to power all the proposed operations was so large that it became an economic proposition to generate all the electricity needed on site, and more besides. Arrangements were made to export any surplus to the National Grid whenever local demand slackened.

About this time, CRESCO Paper Towels, a customer supplied with paper from Oakenclough for almost thirty years, was acquired by Inveresk, causing some concern within the bag factory, happily resolved when plans to build new premises were unveiled in 1962. At the same time, the paper mill was expanded even further in line with Inveresk ambitions to extend their advance into the expanding tissue market. In particular, plans laid in May 1956, to replace the 60 inch machine, came to fruition in 1963 when a huge 120 inch Beloit-Walmsley machine was installed, capable of producing soft tissue at a rate of 2500 feet per minute, and paper towelling in excess of 800 feet per minute 17), five times faster than before. Its MG cylinder was so bulky that it had to be brought in over Harrisend Fell (and, at a later date, taken out by way of Delph Lane).

This huge machine was going to use even more water, so an exploratory hole was drilled close by the mill chimney, revealing the presence of two one inch seams of coal in the underlying strata, but not of water in sufficient quantity. Another hole drilled on the fell slopes above Nanny Brook wood was more successful, but caused no little consternation when a test run dried up the local springs. However, this unexpected reaction proved to be of only temporary duration, and this alternative bore hole proved to be capable of supplying all the extra water needed to keep the mill in production.

The extensive additions made by Inveresk between 1955 and 1963 can be identified by comparing a plan prepared in 1971 (page 63) with the 1912 layout (page 57), since no substantial external change to the buildings took place during the four decades spanning the two world wars. This expansion compensated, to some degree, for the dismay felt by local workers made redundant by the 1962 closure of the Low Mill cotton factory one and a half miles downstream.

In 1967 Inveresk merged with two other companies to become part of a larger group known as British Tissues. A year later Will Jackson retired, handing over the managing director's chair to his son David, who had joined the company a dozen years earlier after seven years in the Royal Navy as a commissioned officer. The future may have looked bright, but a statement on the company's prospects released to the press in March 1971 suggested otherwise. The 220 employees at the paper mill, and the 165 at the conversion factory, were shocked to be told that as a result of 'intense competitive conditions which have coincided with very large increases in raw material, manufacturing and distribution costs over the last three years, the limited operation possible at the Oakenclough mill had proved to be uneconomic.' 18)

Production at Oakenclough came to an end in June 1971. A few people were retained to keep the machinery in working order until it could be dismantled and shipped elsewhere, their work hindered by a summer cloudburst which flooded the premises. Libyan engineers came to oversee the dismantling of the 120 inch machine for shipment to their country. When the factory was finally emptied in 1975, Goldfinger Securities bought up the whole site, enabling smaller firms to buy or rent land or buildings best suited to their requirement.

Gradually, new firms moved in, so that over the course of the intervening years every part of the abandoned mill has been tenanted at some time or another. Their operations are usually discreet and so generate only minor notice in the neighbourhood, but residents came to rue the day that the machine house was given over to the manufacture of ferric chloride, used for metal etching and the treatment of effluent.

Oakenclough Paper Mill
Use of Buildings : 1971

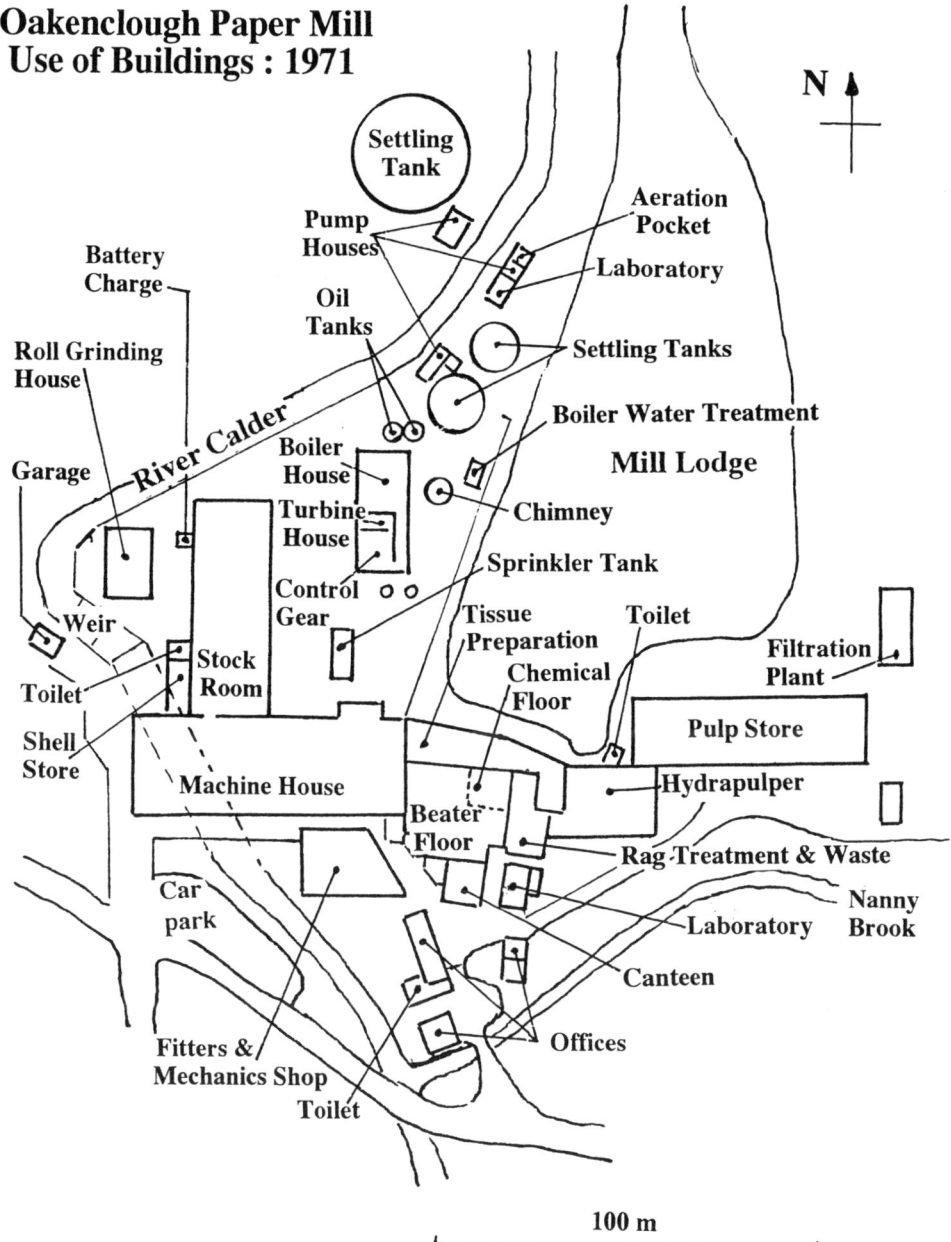

After a series of incidents, worried locals called a public meeting at the Calder Bank restaurant to raise objections concerning the smells emanating from the plant. Their fears were substantiated in Spring 1988 when police, wearing gas masks, evacuated the hamlet because of a serious escape of chlorine 19). Seventeen casualties were taken to hospital and four detained. Reassurances from company spokesmen at a crowded meeting in the village hall at Calder Vale a week later fell on deaf ears, and Wyre borough councillors were urged to take action 20). A change of ownership the following year, and a switch to the manufacture of ferric sulphate (a water industry coagulant), offered a possible solution, but it was all to no avail, because Spring 1993 brought an angry outcry from local residents when sulphuric acid was accidentally spilled into a basement and thick orange fumes poured out of adjacent windows 21). As this was not the only occurrence, the firm responsible, faced with forthcoming tighter regulation, moved out in June 1993, transferring production to another site entirely 22).

In August 1998, six firms were operational on the Oakenclough site, between them providing employment for 38 people. One of the smallest - Speleo Technics - is following in the footsteps of Harold Jackson by satisfying the needs of a specialist market. It is competing successfully in Europe with its range of brightly coloured helmets for climbers and cavers, as well as lamps for cave exploration, and lights for anglers who go fishing after dark.

As for the bag factory, it remains in the business of paper conversion, operated by Walki Wisa Ltd., a member of United Paper Mills, with headquarters in Finland.

Part 3

Water

Dates of Relevance

1853 Fylde Waterworks Company provisionally registered
1860 Decision to proceed
1861 Fylde Waterworks Act (1861) given Royal Assent
1862 Grizedale Reservoir : work commenced
1866 Grizedale Reservoir filled
1874 Fylde Waterworks Act (1874)
1874 Barnacre Reservoirs : work commenced
1876 Grizedale Reservoir : serious leakage
1877 Barnacre Reservoir : southern section filled
1878 Barnacre Reservoir : northern section filled
1883 Grizedale Reservoir : repair complete
1887 Vale Mill purchased by Fylde Waterworks Company
1891 Low Mill purchased by Fylde Waterworks Company
1891 Filter beds added (work complete in 1898)
1891 Fylde Waterworks Act (1891)
1894 Calder river water fed to Barnacre Reservoirs
1897 Fylde Waterworks Transfer Act given Royal Assent
1899 Fylde Water Board Act (1899)
1902 Grizedale Lea Farm purchased by the Fylde Water Board
1903 Grizedale Lea Reservoir : work commenced
1912 Thirlmere water supplied to Calder Vale
1916 Grizedale Lea Reservoir : work abandoned due to war
1918 Grizedale Lea Reservoir : work restarted
1920 Ten week strike
1922 Grizedale Lea Reservoir : ceremonial opening
1935 Mechanical pressure filters introduced into purification system
1949 Grizedale Reservoir : pumps added to raise water to filter level
1949 Barnacre water supplied to Calder Vale
1966 Barnacre water piped to Oakenclough
1973 Water Act combined the region's water companies to create the North West Water Authority
1989 Water Act privatised the water industry

12. The Water Cycle

Given that almost 60% of human body weight consists of water, it is blindingly obvious that life on earth cannot exist without adequate supplies of this essential element. All through the nineteenth century and beyond, the inhabitants of Calder Vale were dependent on the vagaries of nature to satisfy their thirst and desire for cleanliness. River water could have been used, but was subject without notice to the effects of flood, drought, and upstream pollution. Fortunately the hills round about soaked up and stored the rainfall and surrendered it to surrounding wells and springs in a naturally filtered condition. The Kelbrick hills delivered a particularly pure and sparkling liquid, one of its outlets conveniently directed to flow into a stone trough behind School Cottages. Each row of houses had access to some kind of external supply, all needing to be collected and transported by hand-carried pail. Pipes from slopstones led soiled liquid into the river, to be diluted and washed downstream out of sight and mind.

Solid waste was another matter, accumulating in 'ash pits' in petties built behind each row of buildings, awaiting clearance from time to time for use as an organic fertiliser. Experiments were carried out in the 1860s, encouraged by W J Garnett of Bleasdale Tower, to deposit a 'dry earth' mixture on the ordure to improve its texture and quell the odour 1). Towards the end of the century the Garstang medical health officer was recommending the use of peat to sanitise the pail closets in general use, and to render the content suitable for use on the garden 2). He wrote that 'where a sufficient amount of land is attached to a dwelling no better system can exist in a Rural District where water is not available. Such a tub or pail should be emptied at least once a week'. Many of the villagers worked a small plot of land nearby to eke out their livelihood, and would look upon their sludge as a useful low cost soil improver.

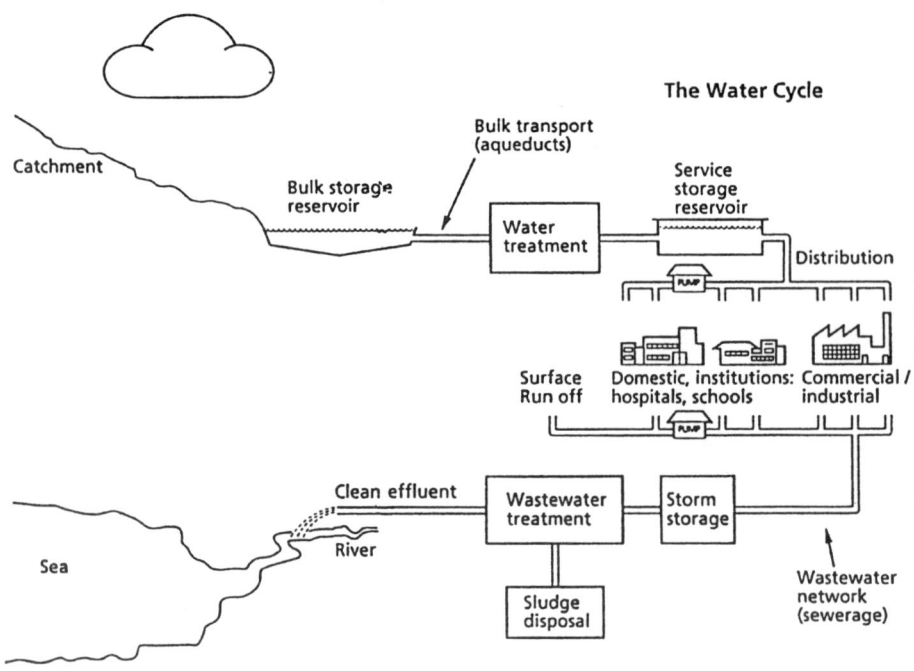

The Water Cycle

The Victorians did not invent the water cycle - ocean to air, air to earth, earth to ocean - how could they? What they did was to improve its efficacy by harnessing, storing, and distributing rain water in an organised manner, and using it to carry effluent away, as shown in the sketch above 3). In the early days, people were happy enough to receive unrefined water, piped into their homes with no filtration or other treatment, but as the years passed by public disquiet grew to demand and expedite improvements. A reflection, in miniature, of the water collection industry of the time was to be found on Barnacre Moor, described in the next chapter.

13. The Grizedale and Barnacre Reservoirs *See page 77 for site plan*

Grizedale Fell, a vantage point on the western side of the Forest of Bowland, gives rise to Grizedale Brook, which takes its course through a picturesque wooded valley well known to hikers as Nicky Nook. Not far south is the River Calder (not to be confused with its namesake in West Yorkshire) which flows through equally attractive tree-lined hillsides encompassing the secluded village of Calder Vale. At Garstang and Catterall respectively these two tributaries join the River Wyre, which wends its way through the centre of the low-lying Fylde district before emerging at Fleetwood. Capturing their flow for distribution through a mains system to serve all the people on the plain was a natural step forward, once the means came to hand.

The arrival of cholera from the East in 1832, a further outbreak in 1848, and particularly the discovery in 1854 (by Dr. John Snow, physician to Queen Victoria) that polluted water was responsible, provided the incentive. Deplorable sanitary conditions in the fast-growing urban areas emphasised the need for ample supplies of uncontaminated water. Entrepreneurs began to look around for catchments of sufficient potential to provide a piped water supply, and in 1853 the Fylde Waterworks Company was provisionally registered 1), though initial enthusiasm was somewhat lacking. Seven years later, a meeting in the Bull Hotel in Preston 2) considered proposals to take water either from the River Brock (yet another Wyre tributary rising in Bleasdale Moors) or from Grizedale Brook. The meeting chose the latter, resolving thereupon to proceed and prepare a prospectus to attract potential investors. The Fylde Waterworks Act (1861) was given the Royal Assent, and the Fylde Waterworks Company, with an initial capital of £60 000, was in business, under the chairmanship of Thomas Langton Birley, Esq., of Carr Hill, Kirkham 3).

In 1862 Grizedale Reservoir was costed at £22 976. 13s. 5d. and work began 4). Two years later, 699 houses along the coastline had been connected to an embryonic mains system 5), but it was not until November 1866 that the reservoir was filled for the first time 6). Within months, a leak had been spotted below the embankment 7), which could be located only by reducing the water level and then digging down to plug the hole from inside. This disaster, combined with an exceptionally dry summer in 1868, compelled the imposition of severe water restrictions, including a daily cut off between 4 p.m. and 6 a.m. 8).

In 1869 the repair was complete and the reservoir refilled 9), but it was obvious that further capacity was required, and an engineer's report in 1873 10) suggested construction of one or more reservoirs near the site of an existing water hole called 'Sconce Tarn' on Barnacre Moor to the south of the Grizedale valley. Work was authorised by the Fylde Waterworks Act of 1874, and Barnacre Reservoir was put in hand once the expected cost of £47 071. 10s. 5d. had been agreed 11). The engineer recommended that the reservoir be divided into two 12), for three reasons:

1) that 'pure' and 'flood' waters could thereby be kept separate, so that when the source delivered discoloured water it could be allowed to settle in the southern portion;

2) that security would still be maintained, should one part spring a leak;

3) that waves generated by the wind would be calmed by the dividing wall.

No serious problems were encountered during construction, and in 1877 Grizedale water was diverted along a newly constructed conduit into the southern part, the northern section coming into use a year later 13).

In the meantime, Grizedale Reservoir had been causing concern, with a severe leak reported in the winter of 1876 14). Two years later, despite repairs, there was still a seepage, probably because concrete had not hardened properly, and the directors seriously considered abandoning the reservoir altogether in 1879 15). A new engineer was engaged, legal proceedings were taken against the previous engineers 16) (settled out of court), and in 1883 the reservoir was once more full, after repairs costing in all £31 946.7s.6d. (nearly half as much again as the original cost) 17).

Other local authorities were casting covetous eyes at Bleasdale Moors, and a meeting in 1875 recorded a possibility that Liverpool Corporation might wish to take water from the River Calder 18). To counteract this threat, Fylde Waterworks bought Calder Vale Spinning Mill in 1887 19) and Calder Vale Weaving Shed in 1891 20), thereby securing the water rights, which they would retain on resale. In 1890 the directors decided to apply to Parliament for confirmation 21), and the Fylde Water Act (1891) gave permission "to divert, collect, impound, and use the waters of the Calder Dyke and Calder River, and the construction of culverts to convey the Calder water to the Barnacre and Grizedale reservoirs".

An indenture confirming the land owner's agreement was sealed in December 1894 22), and in no time at all this additional supply was on tap. Unfortunately, this understanding merely to extract water from the Calder was soon to prove inadequate. In particular, the clear spring water was not kept separate from flood water, resulting in considerable wastage during storm conditions, when the combined water became so muddy it could not be fed into the reservoirs. Other improvements were needed to guard against contamination, so an approach was made to William Garnett, the land owner. He did not want to sell the land, so it was left to arbitrators to decide on compensation which would allow the necessary access to Fylde Water, without interfering unduly with sporting interests 23). During 1912 and 1913 the Calder Dyke was tapped much nearer to its source, the Calder river bed was disentangled from the cart track to the Arbour (where shooting parties took their lunch), and many rivulets were examined and strengthened against future land slip.

It would be too much to expect that an undertaking of such fundamental importance to the locality would be free from criticism. Cleanliness was increasingly the subject of reproach. The source itself was pure enough, but floods, collection, and storage would inevitably entrap foreign matter, so filter beds and ultra fine weave sieves were introduced progressively to the Barnacre outlet between 1891 and 1898 24).

The combination of a leaky reservoir and a rapidly expanding network generated much unfavourable customer comment, bringing the Fylde Authorities together to promote a bill for compulsory purchase 25). Naturally there was initial opposition from the company directors, and the Blackpool Gazette and other local papers made much to-do, but the die was cast when the Fylde Waterworks Transfer Act received the Royal Assent on the sixth of August 1897. Joint meetings were held to oversee an amicable hand over and determine compensation to stock holders, scheduled in the Fylde Water Board Act of 1899.

So it was that the Fylde Water Board came to face the challenge of the twentieth century in place of the Fylde Waterworks Company 26), and be subjected to much the same kinds of criticism for as long as demand continued to outstrip supply. Prior to hand over the need for a further reservoir had been apparent. Water restrictions took their toll in unexpected ways. A press report culled in 1911 tells us that church organs in Lytham fell silent during prohibition periods because of their dependence on water power 27). It was at such times that independent schemes to make up the shortfall would surface, offering to provide a separate non-potable saltwater supply from the sea, quickly forgotten the moment the rain clouds reappeared 28).

Watching over all these activities were the adjacent 136 acres comprising Grizedale Lea Farm, purchased in 1902 29) (the farm buildings were kept in use for various purposes until their demolition in 1915).

Plans were drawn up to create a new reservoir on this farmstead holding more than the existing ones combined, so for such a large project a first priority was to build cottages and lodging houses, with canteen and recreation facilities, to accommodate the workforce (in 1905, 166 of the 300 men employed that year could sleep on site, and 11 horses could be stabled) 30). This laudable concern for workers' welfare was undoubtedly influenced by recent problems at 'Blake's Huts', which had been erected in the first place to house labourers laying the pipe track of Manchester's supply from Thirlmere as it passed through Barnacre, but later came to be occupied by 50 or 60 Fylde Waterworks navvies. In 1892 the unsavoury living conditions became so notorious that the Garstang Rural Sanitary Authority had to intervene to clean up the mess 31).

Seeking the money to pay for this reservoir proved troublesome. The directors were pursuing a 60 year loan, but although the Local Government Board agreed to fund the £137 727 originally required, it insisted on repayment over 30 years 32). It was only after considerable argument and the introduction of the Fylde Water Board Act (1910) that the loan was extended to 40 years.

Work began in earnest on the 27th of July 1903 33), but finance was not going to be the only problem. Geology, weather, and war, would all bring complications, leading to excessive delay. By the time the reservoir was complete in 1922 it was going to cost more than twice the original estimate.

In 1910 a consulting engineer reported: "I have never seen in the course of my experience a Reservoir site on which the rocks were more disturbed and broken up by faults .... [A] member of the clay group which has given much work is a laminated clay sometimes known as Bible Clay or 'Book-leaf Marl'.......The interlaminations of sand and clay render it a formidable deposit from its tendency to absorb water, and thus occasion slips. It is being carefully removed." 34).

Four other kinds of clay were present: a strong yellow clay, a strong heavy black clay, a stony dark clay, and a soft light blue clay. All these were tested over several days under a column of water 105 feet high and were passed as satisfactory. Lashings of water and much heavy spade work would homogenise these into a 'clay puddle' which would be trampled down over porous zones to prevent seepage.

However, further consideration in 1911 led to large areas of clay puddle being removed and underlined with thick layers of concrete 35).

The reservoir site was a busy one. In 1910 there were six steam locomotives traversing the compound 36), and six horses fully occupied carting material from Garstang and Catterall railway station. Inevitably, there were accidents, though none of them were fatal. In 1904 a fall of earth broke a workman's leg 37); in 1906 a brakesman fractured a leg while riding the wagons against regulations 38); and in 1908 a horse named 'Wide-Awake' fractured a hind leg and was off work for ten weeks 39), but incidents such as these were mercifully few, and the fact that no contagion or epidemic swept the site could be ascribed to the wisdom of providing good accommodation at the outset.

Work was well advanced when along came the First World War. The 425 men employed at the outbreak in 1914 dwindled to 73 by July 1916 40) (300 navvies joined the army). In June 1916, the Local Government Board stopped construction 41), and a licence had to be obtained to retain a maximum of 40 men for repair work 42). In times of flood, all these men might be needed to stabilise unfinished banks on the Calder. Redundant equipment and timber were sold off. In June 1917, since only 31 men remained, a fortuitous decision was taken to close six huts, three cottages, the canteen and the mission room (host to many a jolly social gathering) 43). Within days, a terrifying thunderstorm and a direct lightning strike badly damaged the buildings, and would have forced their evacuation anyway. When the Local Government Board gave consent to proceed, six weeks after the war had ended, men were engaged immediately, building up to 228 by June 1919, though some left temporarily to bring in the harvest 44).

August 1919 brought along a severe water shortage, but the 14 foot depth (without leaks) gleefully reported by the newspapers was only one quarter of that intended, and could not yet be released for distribution 45). Local papers continued to report on the levels: 21ft. 6in. in November 1919 46), 24ft. 6in. in January 1920 47), 30ft. 6in. in April 1920 48).

The immediate post war years were marked by a torrent of civil unrest when even policemen went on strike, so perhaps it was not surprising that the 160 men working towards completion downed tools in August 1920, alleging victimisation of their Union Branch Secretary 49), and the site was closed down for ten weeks. The following year a coal strike created difficulties, but the end was now in sight. Finally, on the 31st of August 1922, after nineteen long years, the permanent inlet valve was opened in ceremonial fashion 50), and the following statistics concerning Grizedale Lea Reservoir were released to the press:

Total cost	: £322 727
Available capacity	: 284 million gallons
Area	: 34 acres
Perimeter	: 1.25 miles approximately
Maximum depth	: 49 feet 6 inches
Materials used	: 245 000 tons of clay puddle
	82 000 tons of pitching and beaching
	63 000 tons of concrete.

Men and equipment were transferred to Stocks Reservoir, an even larger project just beginning in the Hodder Valley, and the limelight faded from Barnacre, as the permanent staff of some two dozen or so took over the day-to-day routine. Grizedale Lea was to prove its worth in 1929 when a summer heat wave created a countrywide drought, which the Fylde, after long delay, now had better means to resist.

Stocks Reservoir was opened by Prince George, the future Duke of Kent, on the 5th of July 1932 51), neatly anticipating a further drought suffered elsewhere in 1933, and finally stilling the local clamour for ever more reserves.

In 1935 it was decided to upgrade the Barnacre purification system by replacing the hand washed screens by mechanical pressure filters 52). In 1949 pumps were installed to carry water uphill to the filters from the lower level Grizedale Reservoir 53). Despite drainage and a complete overhaul in 1910/1911, the lack of filtration had kept these waters out of general use for thirty-seven years.

One could be forgiven for thinking that, with all this stored water in the vicinity, Calder Vale would have been an early recipient. Not so! It is true that the 1891 Act did place Fylde Water under an immediate obligation to "construct ....a sewer or drain ....for the purpose of sewering the cottages now erected at Calder Vale", and this was done by connecting the numerous independent outfalls to a discharge point downstream of the Low Mill tailrace.

However, the provision of water to the village was quite another matter, taken up by a sub-committee of the Garstang Rural District Council in 1904 54). Its first idea of utilising local springs was abandoned in 1907 in favour of tapping into the Thirlmere water main 55), which crosses the Calder just south of Low Mill. An agreement with Manchester Corporation was approved by the Local Government Board in 1909 56), but three more years passed before the water was turned on 57).

This arrangement lasted until 1949, when the need to cater for twenty new houses and replace encrusted feeder pipes led to a reappraisal. The benefits of a gravity supply from Barnacre were self evident, so contracts were negotiated with the Fylde Water Board and the agreement with Manchester Corporation terminated on 30.6.1949 58).

At long last the inhabitants of Calder Vale could savour water taken from their own river, a privilege already enjoyed by others for more than half a century. Further upstream on a higher level, fed from their very own header tank atop Barnacre Moor, Oakenclough and the Moorcock Inn were connected in 1966 59).

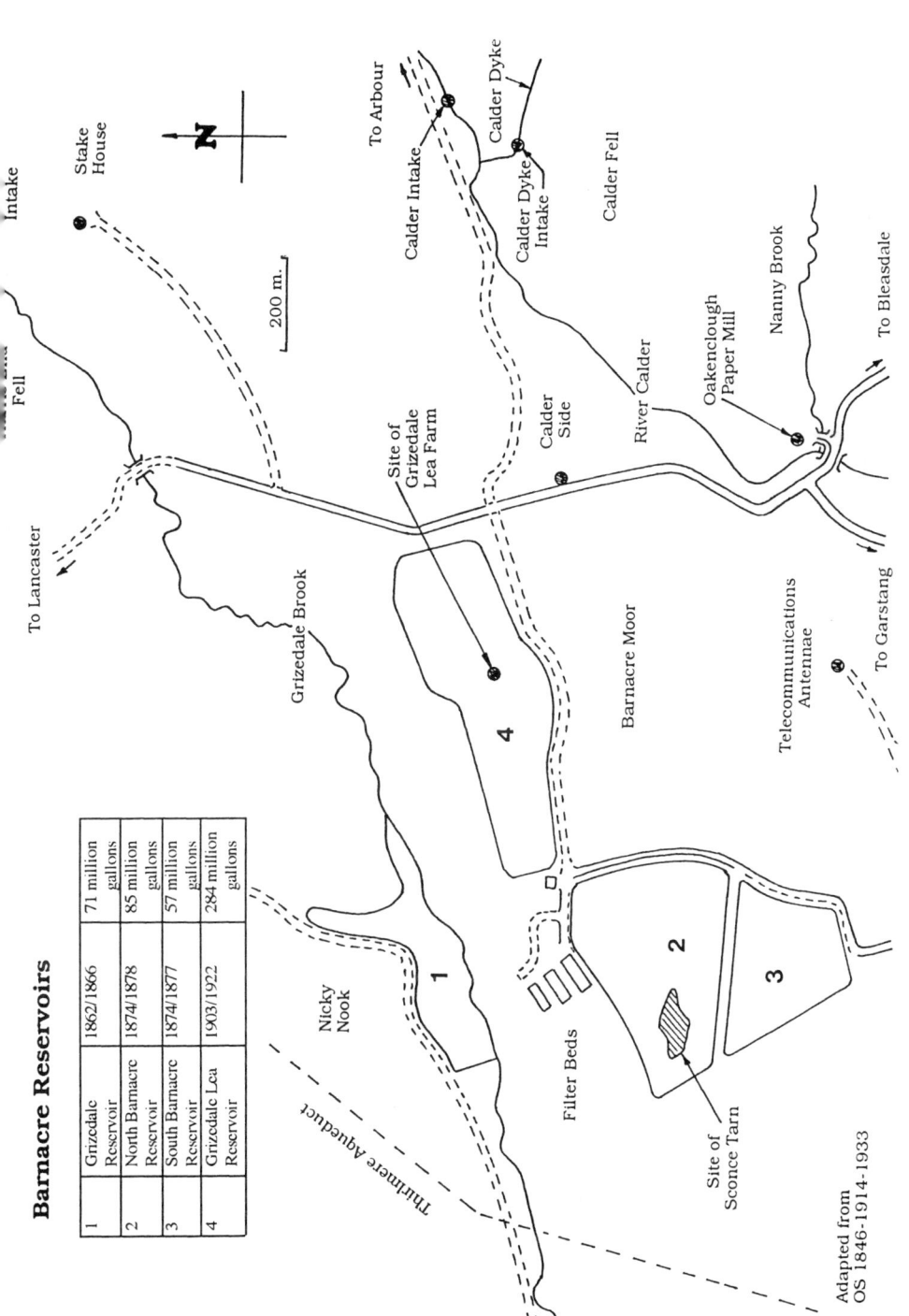

Appendices

Appendix A

Notes and References

Chapter 6 : Calder Vale mills in the nineteenth-century

1) *Fylde Water Bill, 1891* : Appendix D
2) *Lancaster Gazette* : 15 August 1863
3) Lancashire Record Office (hereafter LRO) DDX 1721/1/2, May 1902
4) *Lancaster Gazette* : 3 January, 1863
5) *Preston Chronicle* : 27 March 1886
   Preston Chronicle : 27 August 1887
6) *History of the Fylde Waterworks*, p. 45
7) LRO/WBF/1/4, p. 368
8) LRO/PR 955 (1896)
9) LRO/WBF/2/1, p. 301
10) LRO/RDG/13/1 (1903)
11) LRO/RDG/13/1 (1908)
12) *Skinner's Cotton Trade Directory of the World*

Chapter 7 : Vale Mill : 'The Lappet'

1) Articles of Association of Lappet Manufacturing Company Ltd : Incorporated 23.07.1909
2) Lappet Company handout : 1994
3) Informant : Jim Liver
4) Lappet Company handout : 1994
5) Informant : Jim Liver
6) Informant : Jim Liver
7) *Skinner's Cotton Trade Directory of the World : 1940 - 1941*
8) Vale Mill archives : Wages ledger : 1940 - 1948
9) Vale Mill archives : Wages ledger : 1940 - 1948
10) Vale Mill archives : Wages ledger : 1940 - 1948
11) Vale Mill archives : Wages ledger : 1940 - 1948
12) *Lancashire Evening Post* : 25 October 1956
13) Vale Mill archives : Sales ledger : 1921 - 1966
14) *The Lancashire Textile Industry : 1962*
15) Vale Mill archives : Sales ledger : 1921 - 1966 :
    John Lean included as a customer from 1959 onwards
16) Informant : Bob Quick
17) *The Times* : 21 August 1964
18) *The Times* : 2 July 1968
19) *Yorkshire Post* : 20 November 1981
    The Times : 1 October 1981
20) *Lancashire Evening Post* : 30 January 1996
21) *The Times* : 22 February 1990
    The Guardian : 22 February 1990
22) *Lancashire Evening Post* : 28 April 1993
23) *Financial Times* : 29 March 1996

Chapter 8 : Lappet Satellites

Information in this chapter supplied by Bob Quick

Appendix A (continued)

Chapter 9 : Low Mill

1) *Preston Chronicle*, 2 April 1887
2) *Fylde Water Bill, 1891*, Appendix D
3) *Preston Chronicle*, 6 December 1890
4) *Lancaster Observer*, 25 May 1894
5) *History of the Fylde Waterworks* , p. 149
6) *History of the Fylde Waterworks* , p. 151
7) LRO/PR 955 (1896-1907)
8) Vale Mill archives : Sales ledger 1898-1902
9) LRO/RDG/1/2, 18 February 1897 & 18 March 1897
10) Harris Library, Preston, L 25 MIS
    Lancashire Daily Post, 11 June 1909
11) LRO/RDG 13/1 (1903-1914)
    LRO/RDG 13/2 (1915-1924)
12) Informant : Arnold Whitehead, son of Arthur
13) LRO/RDG 19/1/1914/48
14) LRO/RDG 19/1/1924/32
15) Informant : Arnold Whitehead
16) Informant : Arnold Whitehead
17) Informant : Arnold Whitehead
18) *Skinner's Cotton Trade Directory of the World*, 1954
19) *Lancashire Evening Post*, 25 October 1956
    Lancaster Guardian, 9 November 1956
20) *Lancashire Evening Post*, 4 May 1962
21) Informant : David Jackson

Chapter 11 : Oakenclough Paper Mill

1) Informant : David Jackson
2) LRO/DDJa/2/2 : Goods Bought Ledger : 1832 - 1834
3) LRO/DDJa/1/2 : Sales Ledger : 1832 - 1837
4) *Preston Guardian*, 4 October 1941
5) *Preston Guardian*, 4 October 1941
6) Original Agreement held by David Jackson
7) *The Fylde Water Bill, 1891 : Minutes of Evidence*
8) *The Fylde Water Bill, 1891 : Minutes of Evidence* : page 28
9) LRO/DDJa/2/7 : page 65 : Goods Bought invoice Book : 1891 - 1898
10) LRO/DDJa/2/6 : page 95 : Goods Bought Ledger : 1891 - 1903
11) *Fishing Gazette*, 13 December 1902
12) *Preston Guardian*, 4 October 1941
13) LRO/DDJa/6/1 to 9 : Paper Sample Books
14) *The Times*, 6 & 13 July 1954
15) LRO/RDG/1/33, 22 December 1955
16) LRO/RDG/1/33 & 34, relevant minutes
17) *The Inveresk Paper Group News*, April 1964
18) *Lancashire Evening Post*, 31 March 1971
19) *Lancashire Evening Post*, 30 April 1988
20) *Lancashire Evening Post*, 6 May 1988
21) *Lancashire Evening Post*, 24 February 1993
22) *Lancashire Evening Post*, 22 April 1993

Appendix A (continued)

Chapter 12 : The Water Cycle

1) LRO/DDQ, Letter from Grant King to W J Garnett, 8 August 1866
2) LRO/RDG/18/8 (1896)
3) Reproduced, with permission, from North West Water leaflet reference 120593L

Chapter 13 : The Grizedale and Barnacre Reservoirs

1) *History of the Fylde Waterworks : 1861-1911* (hereafter HFW), p. 6
2) HFW, pp. 14-15
3) HFW, p. 16
4) HFW, p. 23
5) HFW, p. 43
6) HFW, p. 46
7) HFW, p. 49
8) HFW, p. 53
9) HFW, p. 54
10) HFW, p. 64
11) HFW, p. 72
12) HFW, pp. 77-78
13) HFW, p. 98
14) HFW, pp. 78-79
15) HFW, p. 104
16) HFW, p. 115
17) HFW, p. 128
18) HFW, p. 73
19) HFW, p. 145
20) HFW, p. 146
21) HFW, p. 140
22) LRO/WBF/15/2
23) *Lancaster Observer*, 8 December 1911
    Blackpool Times, 2 December 1911
24) HFW, p. 142
25) HFW, pp. 170-171
26) *Preston Herald*, 16 August 1899
27) LRO/WBF/34/1, p. 96
28) *Blackpool Times*, 16 September 1911
29) HFW, p. 261

Appendix A (continued)

30) HFW, p. 308
31) LRO/RDG/1/2, 8 December 1892
32) HFW, p. 300
33) HFW, p. 272
34) HFW, pp. 380-381
35) HFW, p. 382
36) HFW, p. 364
    (a description of the steam locomotives and railway system used
    during the construction of Grizedale Lea reservoir can be found in :
    Lesser Railways of Bowland Forest and Craven Country : see Appendix B)
37) HFW, p. 289
38) HFW, pp. 317-318
39) HFW, p. 338
40) LRO/WBF/34/5 p. 105
41) LRO/WBF/34/5 p. 106
42) LRO/WBF/34/5 p. 105
43) LRO/WBF/34/5 p. 105
44) LRO/WBF/34/5 p. 176
45) LRO/WBF/34/6 p. 8
46) LRO/WBF/34/6 p. 42
47) LRO/WBF/34/6 p. 51
48) LRO/WBF/34/6 p. 61
49) *Blackpool Times*, 25 August 1920
50) LRO/WBF/34/6 pp. 134-139
51) LRO/WBF/37/7
52) LRO/WBF/37/18 p. 13
53) *Blackpool Gazette*, 16 July 1949
54) LRO/RDG/1/5, 5 & 26 May 1904
55) LRO/RDG/1/6, 12 December 1907
56) LRO/RDG/1/7, 4 March 1909
57) LRO/RDG/1/8, 1 May 1912
58) LRO/RDG/1/26, 20 January 1949
59) Garstang Rural District Council minutes, 24 March 1966

Appendix B

Bibliography

Population Census Returns, 1851 to 1891

Thomas W Fox, *The Mechanism of Weaving*, MacMillan & Co Ltd, 1900

Anthony Hewitson ('Atticus'), *Northward*, 1900

Christopher Arthur, *History of the Fylde Waterworks Company : 1861 - 1911*, Blackpool Times, 1911

Harold Catling, *The Spinning Mule*, The Lancashire Library, 1986

Harold D Bowtell, *Lesser Railways of Bowland Forest and Craven Country*, Plateway Press, 1988

Richard L Hills, *Papermaking in Britain : 1488 - 1988*, The Athlone Press, 1988

Michael Winstanley (editor), *Working Children in Nineteenth-Century Lancashire*, Lancashire County Books, 1995

Mike Malley, British Paper Mills : Oakenclough Paper Mill (Excise Number 163), *The Quarterly 21*, January 1997 (*The Quarterly* is the Journal of the British Association of Paper Historians)

Mike Malley, British Paper Mills : Oakenclough Paper Mill between 1845 and 1914, *The Quarterly 23*, July 1997

Appendix C

Cotton Mill employment (1841-1891) as portrayed by the Calder Vale Census Returns

Description/Date	1841 1)	1851	1861	1871	1881	1891
Manager(s)	-	2m	2m	1m	1m	1m
Overlookers	-	4m	6m	4m	3m	4m
Accountant	-	1m	1m	1m	-	-
Bookkeeper	-	1m	-	-	-	-
Bobbiner	-	5m 1f	3m	-	3m	-
Carder	4m 1f	6m 10f	1m 1f	4m	4m	-
Cop Winder	-	1f	2f	-	-	1f
Creeler	-	-	3m	4m 2f	1m	-
Doffer	4m 2f	4m 1f	7m	1m	4m	-
Drawer	5f	1m 5f	1m 4f	3f	2f	1m
Frame Tenter	-	8f	10f	1m 4f	2f	1m
Grinder	-	2m	2m	6m	1m	-
Labourer	-	3m	9m 3f	7m	2m 1f	1m
Loomer	-	-	-	1m	2m	1m
Mechanic	-	-	-	1m	2m	1m
Miscellaneous 2)	3m	2m 2f	1m	7m	-	-
Packer/Shipper	-	1m	1m	1m	-	-
Piecer	-	5m 1f	2m	1m	-	-
Reacher	-	-	-	1f	-	1m
Reeler	1m 16f	10f	6f	16f	8f	-
Rover	10f	2f	2f	5f	8f	-
Self-acting minder	-	-	2m	1m	2m	-
Sizer/Taper	-	1m	1m	1m	1m	1m
Slubber	-	-	1f	1f	1f	-
Spinner	13m 33f	7m 23f	6m 18f	9m 4f	12m 9f	1m
Stripper	2m	-	2m	-	-	-
Throstle Doffer	-	2m	2m 1f	2m	1m	-
Throstle Spinner	-	1m 13f	9f	11f	3f	-
Unspecific	5m 11f	4m 12f	3m 6f	7m 4f	8m 6f	-
Twister	-	2m	-	3m	2m	-
Warper	-	2m 1f	2m 2f	1f	2f	4f
Weaver	-	16m 51f	15m 57f	6m 48f	6m 37f	30m 53f
Winder	-	7f	1m 15f	1m 7f	9f	6f
TOTALS	32m 78f	72m 148f	73m 137f	70m 107f	55m 88f	43m 64f

1) Rudimentary return
2) Miscellaneous includes : Hanker (1841), Maker up (1841), Paper cutter (1841), Heald knitter (1851), Twist thresher (1851), Waister (1851), Cop hooker (1861), Beater minder (1871), Lap carrier (1871), Switcher (1871), Throstle setter (1871)

m = male; f = female

Appendix D

Paper Mill employment (1841-1891) as portrayed by the Oakenclough Census Returns

Description/Date	1841 1)	1851	1861	1871	1881	1891
Manager(s)	John	James + Richard	James + Richard	James	James	Harold
Back tenter				1m		1m
Blacksmith (4)					1m	1m
Beaterman (2)			1m			1m
Bookkeeper						1m
Carter/Wagoner (4)		2m	3m	3m	2m	2m
Commercial Clerk					2m	
Cotton boiler			1m			
Engineer (4)		1m			1m	
Fireman		1m	1m			1m
Joiner (4)	1m	1m			1m	1m
Labourer					2m	3m
Machine tenter		1m	2m		2m	
Paper bag maker				1m 2f	1f	1f
Paper catcher			2m			2f
Paper cutter			1m	1m		1m
Paper finisher			1m		1m	1m
Paper maker	8m	4m	2m	5m	6m 1f	4m 1f
Rag chopper/sorter	1m	1m	4m		1m	1m 2f
Traveller		1m				1m
Willow tenter 3)		1m				
TOTALS	10m	13m	18m	11m 2f	19m 2f	19m 6f

1) Rudimentary return
2) Designated 'mindsa scutcher' in 1861
3) Raw material cleanser
4) Assumed by domicile to be a paper mill employee

m = male; f = female

Appendix E
Glossary

Beam : the cylinder on a loom on which the warp is wound before weaving
Brocade : silken stuff with a rich raised design

Calico : plain white or unbleached cotton cloth
Cambric : fine white linen or cotton fabric
Carder : one who works on a carding engine which combs out & cleans cotton
Cartridge paper : a stout paper generally used for drawing (originally used to make cartridges)
Cellular : an open texture weave
Check : a fabric patterned with small squares
Chintz : printed (often floral and multi-coloured) and glazed cotton fabric
Clipper : one who operates the machine which clips unwanted loops separating elements within each block of lappet patterns
Conversion : as applied to the paper industry, this refers to the addition of coatings or laminates to, and / or impregnation of, the base material to satisfy the ultimate requirement
Cop : a conical roll of thread wound on a spindle
Coucher : one who transfers newly formed paper from its mould to a felt
Creel : 1) the frame supporting bobbins of roving on a spinning mule
   2) the frame supporting cops of yarn to be wound on to the warp-beam
Crêpe : a fine often gauze like fabric, or paper, with a wrinkled texture

Dobby : an attachment to a loom for weaving small figures
Doctor knife : a thin metal blade which closely contacts a roller to accomplish some kind of separation
Doffer : one who removes bobbins or spools from a textile machine
Doria stripe : a striped Indian muslin
Drawer : one who threads the warp through the heald loops

Esparto : a tough wiry grass, native to Spain and North Africa, used to make paper

Felt : in paper manufacture, is a compacted woven fabric of wool or cotton with a raised surface, used to support paper as it translates from a wet to a dry state
Fly : short fibres which escape during spinning
Fourdrinier : the name applied to the normal type of paper machine, after the brothers who financed its early development
Fustian : thick twilled cotton cloth with a short nap

Gabardine : worsted cotton or rayon twill
Gauze : a thin transparent fabric with a loose open weave
Gin : a machine for separating cotton from its seeds
Griffe : a horizontal knife-bar employed in pattern weaving to raise or depress selected healds or heald frames

Heald (or Heddle) : one of the sets of parallel cords or wires carrying loops through which the warp is threaded

Jaconette : a fine waterproof cloth for poulticing

Kraft paper : tough wrapping paper made from sulphate wood pulp (from the German *Kraft* : force, strength)

Lappet : a muslin type cloth with interwoven pattern
Lawn : a fine cotton cloth used for clothes
Leno : an open work fabric, with the warp threads twisted in pairs before weaving
Linen : a cloth woven from flax
Linsey-woolsey : a fabric of coarse wool woven on a flax warp

Marquisette : a sheer fabric used for net curtains
Mercerising : a treatment which gives cotton a silk-like finish, and may also be used to improve dye absorption
MG cylinder : a highly polished, steam-heated, drying cylinder which smooths the one side of the paper in contact
Mule : a spinning machine which automatically produces yarn from rovings (called a mule because it is a hybrid from Arkwright's warp machine and Hargreaves' jenny)
Muslin : a diaphanous cotton fabric used for dresses and curtains

National Grid : a country-wide distribution network of high-tension electrical transmission cables brought about by the creation of the Central Electricity Board in 1926
Noils : tangles and knots combed from woollen fibres

Organdie : a fine translucent cotton muslin, usually stiffened

Petty : an outdoor toilet
Pick : 1) a weft thread
       2) the throw of the shuttle across the loom
Piecer : one who joins together the ends of threads which break whilst being spun or wound
Pirn : a spool of cotton used in a shuttle
Pongee : soft thin unbleached silk with a knotty weave

Rayon : synthetic textile fibre made from viscose (a form of cellulose, the main constituent of plant cell walls)
Reed : a comb like implement to separate the warp and beat up the weft
Reeler : one who winds yarn on to a rotating frame or cylinder

Ripper: one who cuts the loops which separate adjacent blocks of lappet patterns
Rover: one who combines slivers into the rovings to be fed to the spinning machine
Roving: a continuous stream of aligned fibres

Satteen: Satin woven cotton fabric with a glossy sheen
Selvedge: the edge of a cloth woven so as not to unravel
Shed: the opening between the warp threads through which the shuttle carries the weft
Shirtings: fabrics intended for shirt making
Size: a glutinous solution used to :
    1) stiffen and glaze fabrics
    2) reduce water absorption and bind fillers in paper
Slay: the oscillating part of a weaving machine which carries the reed, and may carry other mechanisms
Slopstone: an oblong sandstone kitchen sink, with a drainage hole in its base
Splits: fabrics woven two or more in the width for later separation. Two warp threads are usually omitted to indicate the cutting line

Tackler: one who adjusts and maintains power looms
Taper: an operative in charge of a sizing machine
Temple: a loom attachment which keeps the cloth stretched to its correct width
Tenter: a minder, e.g., machine tenter
Throstle: a device for continuously twisting and winding yarn
Tow: coarse broken bits of flax or hemp fibre
Treadle: a pivoted lever translating motion from one plane to another, used on hand looms to operate the heald frames

Vat: the tank containing the stuff from which paper is made
Velveteen: cotton fabric with a pile like velvet
Voile: a thin semi-transparent dress material

Warp: the threads running the length of a woven fabric
Warper: one who spools yarn from cops on the warping creel to the warp-beam
Weft (or Woof): the threads passing through the warp from selvedge to selvedge
Willow: a machine to carry out preliminary beating, picking, and cleaning operations

Yashmagh: the name for a head-shawl in Saudi Arabia

Index

P : *see photographic insert*

Albert Mill Company : 42, 43
Ashton Brothers : 34

Bag Factory : 55, 61, 62, 64, P
Barnacre Weaving Company : 42, 43, 44
Birley, Thomas Langton : 69
British Tissues : 62

Calder Vale Manufacturing Co : 43
Courtaulds : 34, 35, 36, 38, 39, 40
Courtaulds Textiles PLC : 38, 39
Craig, Bill : 44, 46
CRESCO : 61
Curtis, Richard : 52
Curtis, Thomas : 52

Dryden Engineering : 56
Duke of Kent : 75

Education Act, 1918 : 30

Factory Act, 1833 : 27
Fourdrinier, Henry : 49
Fourdrinier, Sealy : 49
Fylde Water Act, 1891 : 71, 76
Fylde Water Board : 72, 76
Fylde Water Board Act, 1899 : 72
Fylde Water Board Act, 1910 : 73
Fylde Waterworks Act, 1861 : 69
Fylde Waterworks Act, 1874 : 70
Fylde Waterworks Company : 10, 29, 30, 41, 42, 55, 69, 71, 72
Fylde Waterworks Transfer Act, 1897 : 72

Garnett, WJ : 67, 71
Garstang Rural District Council : 60, 76
Garstang Rural Sanitary Authority : 73
Goldfinger Securities : 62

Haines, Joan : 60
Hall, Richard : 55
Hart, Bill : 36
Harrt, Albert & Co : 29
Hewitson, Anthony (Atticus) : 29, 42
Hill, Vivian : 44

Inveresk Paper Company : 60, 61, 62

Jackson, David : 4, 5, 62, P
Jackson, James : 53, 54, 55
Jackson, John : 10, 25, 52, 53
Jackson, John James : 58, 60
Jackson, Jonathan : 10, 25, 27, 29, 41
Jackson, Hal : 60
Jackson, Harold : 55, 56, 58, 60, 64
Jackson, Richard Snr : 10, 25, 27
Jackson, Richard Jnr : 53, 54, 55
Jackson, Will : 60, 62
Jennings, Tom : 45

Lappet Manufacturing Company : 23, 29, **30-40**
Lappet satellites :
- Dye-House, Lancaster : 39
- Hemming, Clitheroe : 40
- Weaving, Carlisle : 39
Lean, John & Sons : 34
Liver, Bert : 32, 33, 34, 36
Liver Bird : 31
Liver, Cecil : 30, 32
Liver, Harold : 30, 32
Liver, James William : 10, 29, 30, 42
Liver, Jim : 32, 33, 34, 36
Liver, Nancy : 32, 34, 36
Liver, Ruth Alice : 30
Liver, Sidney : 30, 32, 34
Local Government Board : 73, 74, 76
Low Mill : 9, 10, 23, 27, 28, 29, 30, 34, **41-46**, 61, 71, 76, 85

Manchester Corporation : 76

National Grid : 61
National Telephone Co : 42

Oakencork : 58, 59
Oakenstrong : 58, 59
Oaklin : 58

Palmolive : 59
Paper Mill : 9, 10, 25, 46, **52-64,** 86, P
Poole, Brian : 36, 38

Quick, Bob : 4, 36

Reservoirs : 10, **69-77,** P
Routledge, Thomas : 54

St John's church : 28, 31
Simpson, Albert : 55
Smeddle, Mr : 44
Snow, John Dr : 69
Speleo Technics : 64
Styal : 25

Ten Hours Act, 1847 : 27

Vale Mill : 9, 10, 23, 25, 26, 27, 28, 29, **30-38,** 39, 41, 71, 85
Velvoride : 59, 60

Walki Wisa : 64
Ward, Tom : 44
Whitehead, Arthur : 43, P
Whitehead, Fred : 43, P
Whitehead, Humphrey : 44, P
Whitehead, James W : 42, 43, 44, P

Yates & Thom : 56

Postscript

Rules
TO BE OBSERVED
By the Hands Employed in
THIS MILL

Attendance :

1. The Overlookers shall be the first to arrive and the last to leave the premises.
2. All persons employed in this Mill shall serve Four Week's Notice before leaving, but the Masters have discretion to discharge any person without notice.
3. Any person presenting themself late for work shall be fined as follows : for 5 minutes 2d., 10 minutes 4d., 15 minutes 6d., &c.
4. Any person leaving their normal workplace, except for Necessary purposes, or Talking with anyone out of their own Alley, will be fined 2d. for each offence.

Personal Behaviour :

5. The Masters expect that all their workpeople will Wash themselves every morning. However, they shall Wash themselves at least twice in the week : on Monday morning and Thursday morning. Any found unwashed will be fined 3d. for each offence.
6. For every Oath or insolent language 3d. for the first offence, and, in case of repetition, the culpable person shall be dismissed.
7. If two persons occupy one Necessary together, they will each be fined 3d. If any Man or Boy enters the women's Necessary he will be dismissed.
8. Any person found Smoking on the premises will be dismissed.

The Workplace :

9. Any person wilfully or negligently damaging Tools or Machinery, or creating unnecessary Waste, will pay to the full value of restitution.
10. Designated persons neglecting to Oil at the appointed times shall be fined 2d.
11. Any person spilling oil on the floor will be fined 2d. for each offence, besides paying for the wasted oil.
12. Weavers shall sweep eight times in the day as directed, when the black face of the suspended Board is turned towards them. Only one quarter of an hour is allowed for each sweep. Spinners shall sweep five times a day. Any neglecting to sweep will be fined 2d. for each offence.
13. Any person hanging anything on the Gas Pendants will be fined 2d.

Finally :

14. The Overlookers are responsible to the Masters for ensuring that these rules are strictly observed.
15. Any person wilfully damaging this Notice will be dismissed.

July 1847

In the absence of nineteenth-century rules for the Jackson cotton mills, the set of regulations reproduced above has been adapted from contemporary notices displayed elsewhere. Similar stipulations might equally well have applied in Calder Vale.